TWAYNE'S WORLD AUTHORS SERIES

A Survey of the World's Literature

Sylvia E. Bowman, Indiana University

GENERAL EDITOR

GREECE

Mary P. Gianos, Detroit Institute of Technology

EDITOR

Takis Papatsonis

TWAS 313

Takis Papatsonis

Takis Papatsonis

By KOSTAS MYRSIADES

West Chester State College

Twayne Publishers, Inc. :: New York

Library of Congress Cataloging in Publication Data

Myrsiades, Kostas.
  Takis Papatsonis.

  (Twayne's world authors series, TWAS 313. Greece)
  1. Papatsōnēs, Takēs Kōnstantinou, 1895–
PA5610.P353Z8   889′.1′32   74–6370
ISBN 0–8057–2669–1

MANUFACTURED IN THE UNITED STATES OF AMERICA

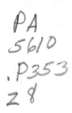
To the generations on either side of me

My parents and my children

Contents

About the Author

Kostas Myrsiades was born in Samos, Greece and was educated in the United States where he has resided since the age of eight. Having entered Iowa University as a medical student, he received both a B.S. and a B.A. there and spent a year at that university's medical school. He went on to study comparative literature at Indiana University, where he earned his M.A. and Ph.D. degrees, and studied modern Greek language and literature at the University of Athens, Greece. An assistant professor of English at West Chester State College, he is currently a visiting professor at Pierce College in Athens where he teaches in the modern Greek studies program. He is a book reviewer for *Charioteer* and *Books Abroad* and has published translations of the poems of Kostas Karyotakis.

Preface

Takis Papatsonis, though a poet of major significance in modern Greek letters, is one whose works have gone largely unread in his own country and untranslated abroad. No critical study of the body of his poetry has been done. This study is the first to have seriously applied the tools of modern criticism to the poet's work. Thus, Papatsonis's poetry still lacks any concise evaluation of its nature and scope; the poet himself has only a hazy notion of how many poems he has published and where. Because of the dearth of information on the subject, the author of this study has undertaken the task of locating the poetry, placing it in chronological order, and creating a context in which the poetry could be effectively analyzed.

Throughout the bulk of Papatsonis's 224 poems, 150 essays, and six prose works, the poet reveals a particular fondness for ancient and medieval Greek and Latin, though he himself disclaims—beyond the great impact made on his work by Dante, Plotinus, the Bible, and to some extent Cavafy—any specific influences. His poetry, however, is heavily impressed with overtones of the Catholic services and with an extensive use of Latin ecclesiastical terminology and dogma. As a result, he has been called not only a religious poet, but more particularly a Catholic one. As this study demonstrates, however, the assumption that Papatsonis's poetry is necessarily Catholic is misleading, for his work is, if anything, religious in the metaphysical sense—in the tradition of T. S. Eliot—and related to the mainstream of European literature by its ties to the Hebraic world of the Bible, the classical world of both Plotinus and Greek mythology, and the medieval world of Dante. The analysis of his poetry and prose in this book takes account of Papatsonis's highly individualized, sometimes idiosyncratic integration of these diverse elements in his poetry and of the poet's technical mastery of his medium which permitted him in the composition of his masterwork *Ursa Minor* in 1944 to join his varied compositional strands to a unified whole deeply infused with an intense poetic vision.

As a first study of the poet's work, this book attempts to apply a variety of critical approaches to elucidate the poetry. Chapter 1 outlines the background which the poet brought to his poetry and furnishes a general overview of the poet's career and its development, providing a concise idea of the periods into which Papatsonis's work falls. Chapter 2 analyzes the theme that most completely permeates the poet's work, using selected poems which most clearly express the poet's developing conception of that theme. Focusing solely on the poet's longest and most richly devised work, *Ursa Minor*, Chapter 3 is a more intense analysis of the major theme of Papatsonis's career, a theme which pervades the dense fabric of that poem.

Stylistic analysis supplements contextual and thematic analysis in Chapter 4, where the poet's compositions are viewed strictly in terms of the stylistic devices and the multilayered imagery which is typical of Papatsonis's most mature poetry. Relying once again on *Ursa Minor* as the most representative and most carefully crafted of the poet's works, the concluding Chapter 5 takes a comparative approach and explores the philosophical nature of Papatsonis's poetry as it is rooted in his study of other religious poets and philosophers.

I would like to acknowledge with gratitude the help of Willis Barnstone of Indiana University, not only for his aid with this manuscript, but for his deep humanity and concern in matters ranging well beyond his duties as a mentor and a scholar. A special acknowledgment of my indebtedness must be extended to the poet himself, Takis Papatsonis, for his willingness to provide me both with his time and any materials in his possession necessary to this study. I would like to thank Kimon Friar for introducing me to the poet and for his help during his residence at the School of Letters, Indiana University, in the summer of 1972, as well as for encouragement during my stay in Athens. For their devotion to a cause very much related to the successful completion of this book, that of academic freedom and professionalism in the American university system, I am exceedingly grateful to professors John Turner and Philip Rudnick of West Chester State College. I would like to express my appreciation also to Alexander Skevi, Alexandrian expatriate and language specialist, for his unflagging optimism, and to Mary Gianos for

Preface

her help in dealing with numerous editorial problems. Finally, a special thanks to Linda Suny Myrsiades who read, typed, and stylized this manuscript innumerable times while at the same time keeping Yani and Leni quiet.

All translations in this book are the author's own unless otherwise specified in the text. A number of poetry translations, indicated by a single asterisk, are taken from Kimon Friar's collection *Modern Greek Poetry*. For permission to use these translations, the author is indebted to Simon and Schuster. For permission to quote from his unpublished translations, indicated by a double asterisk, I would like to thank Kimon Friar himself.

KOSTAS MYRSIADES

Vourliotes, Samos, Greece

Chronology

1895 Born in Athens on January 30.

1913 Published first poems, "Military Songs," in *Akropolis*. Received a B.A. in French from the French Institute of Athens.

1914 Joined Ministry of Economics.

1920 Awarded Knight of the League of Honor, France.

1925 Awarded the Order of Polonia Aestituta.

1927 Followed courses in economics at the University of Geneva.

1930 Attended the League of Nations as representative of Greece. Began negotiations at the Greek-German Trade Treaties Conferences which lasted until 1939.

1933 Published the first translation into Greek of T. S. Eliot's "The Wasteland" in *Kyklos*.

1934 Published *Selection 1*.

1935 Began writing a weekly column in *Kathemerine* which he continued until 1940. Married.

1940 Published *Verses of Exile, The Way of the Cross*, and *A Portion of Noon*, translations of works by Paul Claudel.

1941 Became Deputy Chairman of the Commercial Bank of Greece, a post he still holds.

1944 Published *Ursa Minor*.

1946 Published *Three Poems of Louis Aragon*, translations of works by Aragon.

1949 Began negotiations as the Greek representative at the General Agreement of Trade and Traffic Meetings in England and France which continued until 1955.

1953 Became Vice-Chairman of the Board of the National Art Gallery, where he served until 1966.

1954 Became Secretary General of the Ministry of Economics, a post he held for one year. Attended the meeting of the Organization of European Economic Cooperation as the Greek representative.

1955   Became General Secretary in the Undersecretariat of the Press in the Ministry of Foreign Affairs for one year. Became Vice-Chairman of the Board of the National Theater of Athens, in which position he served until 1964.

1957   Published translations of *Anabasis* by Saint-John Perse and *Tamerlane* by Edgar Allen Poe.

1962   Published *Selection 2*.

1963   Published *An Exercise on Mt. Athos* and wrote "A Triptych from Dante's *Paradiso*."

1964   Became Vice-President of the Greek Society of Aesthetics, until 1969 when he was made President.

1965   Published *Moldawalachia in Myth* and wrote "Dante Alighieri (1265–1965)." Awarded Commander of the Order of George I of Greece.

1966   Published *The Four Cornered Earth I*.

1967   Made permanent member of the Academy of Athens.

1968   Published "Miscellany and Notes on the Holiday of August 15," "Lights from the Grave," and "Concerning Paul."

1969   Published "Schicksalsverbundenheit."

1970   Published *Friedrich Hölderlin: 1770, 1843, 1970* and *National Revolution: Solomos, Calvos*.

1972   Published *Where There Is a Garden*.

CHAPTER 1

An Overview: 1895-1974

I Life and Times

P ANAYIOTIS (Takis) Papatsonis was born January 30, 1895,
in Athens of Catherine and Constantine Papatzonis and was
a descendant of a historical family which played a role in the
Greek War of Independence. His great-uncle, Demetrios Papatzonis, whose name appears as an entry in the *Great Greek Ency-
clopedia*, befriended the hero Theodoros Kolokotronis, while the
poet's grandfather, Panayiotis, was an avid supporter of King
Otho, the first king of modern Greece. The Papatzonis family's
role during the revolution and its aftermath was of some importance in the Messinian area of the Peloponnesus, for members of
that family had resided in Messinia from as early as 1600 and had
supplied governors for Emblakion, a district of forty-five villages,
during the Turkish occupation.

On his mother's side, Papatsonis was descended from the Mar-
quesa di Bartoli of Ancona, a member of an ancient Italian Catholic family from whose ranks emanated a number of ecclesiastics.
He claims descent as well from the Byzantine ruler Komnenos,
from whom he borrowed his early pen name "Nobilissimus."
Though he later reverted to the use of his natural surname, he
changed the "z" to an "s," spelling it "Papatsonis," to concur with
its proper pronunciation. Married into the Empedocles family,
the founders of the Commercial Bank of Greece, the poet was
affiliated through his wife's mother with the Petrocchios, a successful commercial family engaged in cotton trade and presently
settled in Chios, though originally an old family from Veria. Both
his wife's parents were British subjects and her upbringing, like
his own, was essentially aristocratic. The marriage produced one
child, a daughter, Maria-Catherine, who is married to Alexander
Coundouriotis, a diplomat presently serving as the Greek consul

in Chicago. He has three grandchildren, Andrew, Helen, and George, whose ages range from seven to twelve.

Papatsonis's aristocratic upbringing explains to some extent the poet's preoccupation with esoteric themes and stylistic refinement in his poetry. He might well be characterized as an almost delicate poet, one who, faced with the terrors of war and the brutalities of man to man, retreated into himself, into ever more exquisite images and often into surreal visions which issued forth in wonder rather than in horror. His Italianate background, on the contrary, explains his predilection for Latin phrases and for Latinate sentiments such as occur in the Catholic services. It has also conditioned his visual imagery, which, however personal and lofty, is concretely based, much as esoteric Catholic theology is consubstantiated with the physical aspects of Christ's passion in the Mass.

In his youth, Papatsonis studied French at the University of Athens and at the French Institute of Athens and was granted a B.A. in French by the Institute in 1913. He continued his language studies, taking Latin at the University, Italian at the Italian Institute of Athens, and studying Portugese, Spanish, and German on his own. His training in languages led to his later introduction through his translations of a succession of foreign literary figures to the Greek cultural scene. Both the extent of his cultural background and his eclectic taste are expressed in the variety of works he translated from the German, French, Spanish, and English, including the first translation into modern Greek of T. S. Eliot's "The Waste Land" in 1933 (preceding by three years Seferis's celebrated translation of that poem), and numerous translations of works by Claudel, Poe, Jimenez, Artaud, Christina Rossetti, Moerike, Anouilh, Baudelaire, Mistral, Breton, Hölderlin, Aragon, Saint-John Perse, Jarry, Joyce, and Ruskin.

In 1922 Papatsonis's formal studies at the University of Athens culminated in a degree in law and political science. He continued his studies in 1927 through attendance at courses in economics at the University of Geneva. In 1914 as a student at the University of Athens, he joined the Ministry of Economics, serving there first as Secretary and Chief of his section, and later as Director of Tariffs and Treaties, General Director, Counsellor of the High Court, Special Counsellor for Economics, and from 1954 to 1955 as Secretary-General of the Ministry. In 1955 he joined the Ministry of Foreign Affairs as General Secretary of the Undersecretariat, a post he held for one year.

As a representative of his government in economic affairs, Papatsonis participated in a number of international meetings, including the League of Nations in 1930, the Greek-German Trade Treaties Conferences from 1930 to 1939, the General Agreement of Trade and Traffic Meetings in England and France from 1949 to 1955, and the meeting of the Organization of European Economic Cooperation in 1954. He also negotiated economic agreements for the Greek government in Havana, Belgrade, Istanbul, Bucharest, Prague, Berlin, Rome, and Paris.

Papatsonis holds a number of decorations awarded for participation in government negotiations relating to economic matters, among them the Order of St. Sabba, Yugoslavia, 1921; the Order of Polonia Aestituta, 1925; the Crown of Italy, 1924; Knight of the League of Honor, France, 1920; and Commander of the Order of George I of Greece, 1965. Beyond his government service, he has been active since 1941 in the commercial world in his capacity as the continuing Deputy Chairman of the Commercial Bank of Greece, a post he assumed by special permission of the Greek government when his father-in-law, a British subject, left Greece for South Africa.

Experienced in economic affairs, Papatsonis has written a number of moderately influential articles on economics, published over a period of forty years. An area in which he exercises considerable prowess, economics is a subject which he holds second only to literature in his writings. His activities in the Ministry of Economics and in the banking world, as well as his essays in the field, have led to his reputation as a prominent spokesman in economics and finance, and indicate the range of interests and talents he brought to his poetry.

It may well have been Papatsonis's interest in such a socially based field as economics which prevented him from becoming a completely solipsistic poet (a threat which one is always aware of in Papatsonis's work), for his poetry, though neither expansive nor socially oriented, is at its best concerned with the common fate of a people, with universal themes that only a man responsive to larger questions could treat. A scientific and concrete discipline of great complexity, economics may also have reinforced Papatsonis's bias toward concrete and intricately devised visual imagery in his poetry.

Involved in the preservation as well as the creation of art, Papatsonis has functioned in various capacities as an artistic conscience in Greece. Having served as the Vice-President of the Greek Society of Aesthetics since 1964, he was made President in 1969; he was Vice-President of the Board of the National Art Gallery from 1953 to 1966, and Vice-Chairman of the Board of the National Theater of Greece from 1955 to 1964. Papatsonis was made a member of the Group of Twelve (an association of artists which awarded the most prestigious literary prize in Greece) in 1961, though he resigned with Elytis in 1963, and the group itself was abolished by the present Greek regime in 1967. In 1967 he was awarded the highest position a literary man may fill in Greece with his election to the Academy of Athens.

Widely travelled, proficient in seven languages, and versed in both the arts and the sciences, Papatsonis in his career has, one notes, extended himself well beyond the purely literary arena. He has been considered, as a result, among the most learned of modern Greece's contemporary poets, joining a list that includes Kazantzakis, Sikelianos, Seferis, Elytis, and Ritsos.

II A Poet of the Thirties

Though Papatsonis's poetic career extends from 1913 to the present, the twenty-year period from 1930 to 1950 contains the bulk of his most important poetry and prose. It was during these twenty years that he produced over half of his entire poetic output and almost two-thirds of the poetry which he considered worthy of inclusion in his two volumes of collected poems. Within this twenty-year period, all but two dozen poems were written during the eleven years between 1933 and 1944, a period which culminates in *Ursa Minor* of 1944, in which Papatsonis combines all the themes of his previous years and reaches the height of his poetic career. From 1913 to 1929, Papatsonis had produced only sixtynine poems, over half of which he later rejected from his collected poems as childish exercises; after 1944 he produced only fortyfour poems, most of which were written before 1954, and never equalled his work of the thirties and early forties. Thus, in spite of numerous differences between Papatsonis and other poets of the thirties, and in contradiction to the prevailing critical opinion

[18]

which places him as a poet of the twenties (the period of Karyo-takian pessimism),[1] he must be considered a product of the later era.

The poetry of the early part of the century, when Papatsonis first began to write, was characterized by the poetry of Kostas Varnalis (b. 1884), as Linos Polites describes in his *A History of Modern Greek Literature*: "The spirit of destruction which in Varnalis sprang from his ideology (and which appears late in his work), was to be a part of the personality, and an essential element in the poetry of later poets, born in the last decade of the nineteenth century (or a little before), who were to begin to make an appearance during the First World War." [2]

This destructive element, however, never occurred in Papat-sonis's poetry, based on a deep-seated religiosity uncharacteristic of the era (1912–1922), and moving toward a highly personal style which was less lyrical and more free in its form than earlier poetry. An optimistic poet of faith, Papatsonis shared with Takes Barbas, George Douras, and Joseph Eliyah a minority form of poetry which in its attitude was not typical of its time. The poetry of the twenties was characterized rather by Karyotakes's poetry, which celebrated the inglorious, the insignificant, and even the absurd, elements lacking in Papatsonis's work. This was a genera-tion immersed in a cult of decadence stressing the inadequacy of the poet, and, as Politis observes, "Papatsonis . . . though of the same generation, is outside that monotonous atmosphere of de-cadence and disbelief." [3]

In the thirties, however, came George Seferis's "Turning Point" (1931), and the "narcissistic ego" [4] which dominated the poetry of this time changed to Seferis's "we," a point of view Papatsonis characteristically adopted. Papatsonis, like Seferis in his *Mythis-torema*, by 1935 also had abandoned strict meter and rhyme to create his own personal style in free verse. It was in the thirties, too, that surrealism was introduced to Greece with Andreas Embiricos's publication of *Furnace* (1935), a work which had a substantial impact on Greek letters.[5] Papatsonis, well ahead of his times, had adopted surrealism even earlier than others of his period, writing poems such as the surrealistically–tinged "Passions of Artemis One Saturday" in 1923, and "The Sluggish of Mind" in 1933, the former before Breton wrote his first manifesto in

1924, and the latter before Breton's work was introduced to Greece by Embiricos:

In passage here a flock of birds
brought us a message from the North, but we turned a deaf ear.

And the Quails in their color of ash reflected the icebergs,
but we were not only deaf—we set snares
and fired upon them and wanted to eat them.
And who? It was we—we who, having awaited
so impatiently the message from the North,
became blind, and not understanding it had come,
fired upon them, wounded them, chased them away.

I do not deny that the flocks were transient,
but we neither loved nor revered their weariness
or their exhaustion; and once they were gone
there fell upon us suddenly a compassion and weight
    of the spirit
for the ungracious act, the evil assault;
and behold, we remained the awkward ones,
the sluggish of mind to discern apparitions,
desolate, with no message from the North,
with our accustomed *mea culpa*
and our profitless self-accusation.

("The Sluggish of Mind") *

Papatsonis, feeling a closeness to the spirit of surrealism, was driven to write an article in 1945 in *Nea Grammata* (a magazine which began its career, as did Papatsonis, as a reaction against Karyotakianism) explaining his psychic affinities to the movement:

Even though I feel so near to surrealism, surrealism does not feel the same toward me. It seems that an inexorable chasm separates us. And this is perhaps the so-called religiousness or neo-Christianism in my poetry. I fear, however, that this might cause great misunderstanding. If I have often chosen to frame the Mystery that surrounds man (I accept it firmly, and perhaps it is along with Nature my most important poetic motive) in the symbols of a beautiful, venerable, and ancient myth—the only one that had the fortune to evolve physiologically alive, in other words in the movements of life, over a period of two or four (let us take the Jewish teaching) thousand years—I do not find it to be such a great aesthetic false step that it would make me a scapegoat of the world of living art. The animosity against dead dogma—against conventional ethics which wither life—I feel justly throbs in these antipoetic verses. But my soul does not tell me to forsake my settling and my wandering within thick gardens which for so many centuries remained almost exclusively the havens of all Art, since from there wells my poetic impulse. The meaning, however, of my poetry, if anyone wishes to look at it closely, is another and the core of it is another: eroticism, perhaps willingly placed in nature and the universe and wrapped in the indestructible mystery of existence. This belief of mine is largely that which places me beside surrealism, psychically, whether surrealism accepts it or not.[6]

His objections to the surrealist ethos, however, were based on his own need to maintain contact with the common man in his poetry, a contact which expressed, in however limited and personal a manner, the poet's own appreciation of the social value of art:

If I am not mistaken, the content of great meaning is for poetry to identify with life and as such to become the common property of all mankind. In truth this is a good ideology; theoretically it is very sound since all men and the appropriate senses have the right to enjoy the beautiful comfortably and intensively. Who, however, can persuade me that this is not in hard reality a utopia? The advocates of this philosophy, the surrealists, will consider me lesser than all other men because I see the tragic end of their own creations, even the most direct and indisputably beautiful ones. How foreign and distant they remain for the majority of people and how many desperate incomprehensibilities and disturbances they give birth to. It is truly an aristocratic and magical poetry. To say that all of these poets are yet unqualified and that the whip, propaganda, intimidation, or mockery will bring them before the feet of the beautiful in a hurry, I am not able to do. These means seem to me to be so medieval and barbarous. If such means are sufficient for dictators and their machinery in order to prescribe the lies of their ideologies, they are completely unsatisfactory and unfitting to prescribe a luminous truth. They lack nobility, and they are far from ideas like those of Beauty, Freedom, and the Joy of Life. Although in other cases the theories of collective art can be permanent in choreography or in entertainment, I cannot accept them in the art of poetry where the theme is not purified.[7]

III *Poetry: 1910–1919*

Papatsonis's poetry, as the poet himself has expressed,[8] does not fall into easily definable periods, but is all of one piece, developing from the simple to the complex, from the unrefined to the mature. Inspirational pieces written to express a particular welling of emotion at a particular time, the poems are conceived of by the poet as equally important, for each filled a personal emotional gap at the time it was composed. Except for *Ursa Minor*, a work which holds an especially important place in the constellation of Papatsonis's poetry, his work cannot, as a result, be easily divided into periods, though a tentative consideration of the poems in ten-year groupings reveals the growing maturity and developing power of the poet, qualities which culminate in the poetry of the thirties and the early forties.

As precursors to the period of the thirties, Papatsonis's poems from 1910 to 1920 demonstrate a preoccupation with themes similar to those used in his mature poetry, themes which are explored over the whole period of his career as continuing strains in his work. From his earliest verses, published in the years 1913–1914, Papatsonis begins to express his lifelong fascination with themes related to the destiny of man's soul and the majesty of God ("And Peace on Earth," "Ascetic Christmas"). Fearful of the Day of Judgment, he seeks forgiveness in order to enter Paradise, turning to God and especially to the Virgin Mother to intercede on his behalf ("To My Lady and Madonna," "Hymn to the Dead"):

> In all speed help me, assist me my Fearful King!
> You who save each of your chosen, lest you view my
>   state.
> Deliver me pure Fount, my Master and King!
> . . . .
> Let me not be lost in this horrid phantasmagoric Fire
> but let me come to your right side where
> the holy sheep graze, far from every somber evil.
>   ("Hymn to the Dead," 19–21; 31–33)

Papatsonis introduces in this period a major theme into the body of his poetry, an interest in a feminine presence as an intervening force between himself and God. This feminine presence (analyzed in depth in Chapters 2 and 3) takes on a radically different aspect in later poems, being transmuted into classical forms in the myths of Artemis, Aphrodite, and Kallisto, though remaining even there a celestial lady to whom the poet looks for guidance, courage, and hope in times of despair.

In 1914 Papatsonis published in *Akropolis* nine twelve-to-sixteen-line poems, which he grouped under the title "Military Songs." The poems glorify the Greek soldiers who fear none but who are feared by all ("The Heroes"). At times they speak of the king who will lead Greece to victory ("Our King"), of praise for the Motherland ("Inciting"), and of those who gave their lives for Her ("For Their Repose on Our Repose"). The simplistic themes are supported by an almost childish vocabulary and uncomplicated rhyme schemes. Like "And Peace on Earth," which rhymes *a a, b b, c c*, the military songs are written in simple rhyme patterns such as *a b b a, c d d c, e f f e*, and *a a b b, c c d d, e e f f*.

Having omitted these poems from both volumes of his collected poetry, the poet has since rejected them as silly patriotic exercises. But even in these minor patriotic renderings, some more mature Papatsonis themes are to be seen. The intensity of his patriotism, for example, is expressed through a comparison to his faith in the Virgin Mary in "The Heroes." Courage is linked to the grace of God in "Supplication," as both attributes are necessary to a meaningful victory. And hope throughout the "Military Songs" ("For Their Repose on Our Repose," "Triumphal Song," "Supplication," "Inciting") is explored as a virtue critical to man's endeavors, a theme which recurs not only in Papatsonis's later poems, but more significantly in a number of essays written from 1915 to 1965 on Dante's *Paradiso* and in his *Ursa Minor* (1944), a work based on the Dantean triad of faith, hope, and love.

The same year as the "Military Songs," the poet published eight other poems, stressing again themes which were to continue in his poetry. Two poems dealt with the Virgin ("To My Lady and Madonna," "My Rosary"), while six others treated related religious themes. In "Holy Wednesday" the young poet expresses his awe of God and his repentance for the sinful life he leads. He sees himself in "Christmas Vigilance" as outside the gate of God and fears lest Satan overpower him:

My eyes' sight is afflicted
by the bitterness of sad tears
which I the sinner heap up on a multitude of other
tribulations, but this is most horrid—instead of
    a devotional festival
I erect a hesitant beast to proclaim a
harmonic service, Divine Goodnesses's laudation
with foolish stagnation I accept
the Master, the Alpha and Omega of Christianity.
Mercy for the wild race's violent uproar
shook even my inner blessedness's calm,
and menaced, I feel my God's curse,
and Mary's Offspring is from me withdrawn.
I the Unassisted Hermit tremble lest I err
lest I unite with mortal warriors and become
Satan's companion; then I will chant
not a Christmas hymn but a dirge.
           (9–24)

In the six poems of 1915, the poet treats the life of Christ—a subject popular with him over the course of his career—focusing on the events of His birth and His sufferings as indicative of a model from which man may draw sustenance in his own life. The two poems of 1916, on the contrary, begin to probe the mixture of erotic and ecstatic love which was to dominate *Ursa Minor*, his major work of the forties. In "Mary of the Afternoon," for example, he speaks of the presence of his love in a night filled with God, a theme to become quite common in his poetry:

And there will gush forth as if from a Fountain
the Mountainous One, dew's Lightning
as if the evening sky were torn
and she appeared and was beloved.
No one in the West has
greater love for her when she disperses
peace, spreading
for multitudes dreams, speaking lovingly.
           (5–12)

In the next two years Papatsonis published only one poem, "Poeta Afflicta," 1917, in which he pursues the feeling of isolation which permeates his "Christmas Vigilance"; he again laments his marginal existence on the periphery of a world of which he is not a part, crying out, "Oh, how my loneliness tires me / when it presents dark extermination" ("Poeta Afflicta," 27–28).

The year 1919 marks the end of Papatsonis's apprenticeship. While previously he had written small rhyming verses averaging about twenty-five lines apiece, his poems now become more lengthy, avoid rhyme completely, and begin to make use of more complicated imagery. "Virgin's Litanies," 1919 (his earliest long poem, 222 lines), while it is essentially a shallow piece reminiscent in its unpracticed manner of the poems of the earlier decade, provides a good example of the advances made in this year. No more than a panegyric on the Virgin expressed in a devout and religious manner, the poem exhibits, nevertheless, all three qualities of the poet's new style:

> *Stella Matutina, ora pro nobis.*
> Morning star, you illuminate Gardens with roses,
>   dawn's luxury,
> morning star and mystic Rose, in the end Reversion
>   returns,
> wealth of Solomon. An embroidered custom of
> all roses, all Narcisuses, you awake with the sight of all
>   the paradises
> of the Hebrew theological lustfulness; what Garden
>   I wonder
> can equal this Rose before which all scions withdraw.
> What garden hidden under odoriferous shades
> perishable delights, loves' couples, or idols, or
>   Hamadryads
> can ever reach the White Rose's envied virginity,
> so all-immaculate that even the Archangelic Lily
> seeks caresses from this Rose.
>   (192–203)

The Virgin in this poem is compared to a rose ("a wide many-leafed flower like a divine Heart," 64), an image the poet was to use extensively in *Ursa Minor* to refer to Beatrice, and an image Dante himself uses for the Virgin. The stars ("like a despotic Cross, / all hope, all diamonds, all longing," 180–181), as in both *Ursa Minor* and the *Paradiso*, become images of hope, and for the first time the poet uses Latin phrases extensively ("O vas spirituale, ora pro nobis," "Vas honorabile, ora pro nobis," "vas insigne devotionis, ora pro nobis," "Rosa mystica, ora pro nobis,"

"Turris Davidica, ora pro nobis," "Turris eburnea, ora pro nobis," "Domus aurea, ora pro nobis," "Foederis circa, ora pro nobis," "Janua coeli, ora pro nobis," "Stella matutina, ora pro nobis," "Regina Sacratissimi Rosarii, ora pro nobis"), a technique which carries over to many of his other poems.

Papatsonis continued, however, to publish poems more in line with the small poems of the preceding years. In these pieces (four in all) he merely reworked old themes and polished his style, expressing in the best of them a desire for the calmness and serenity that issues forth when one trusts oneself to God. In "To a Young Girl Brought Up in a Nunnery" the poet reflects on a young novitiate who resides in calm amidst the howling winds of winter, while in "The Ship" a sailing vessel serves as a vehicle for man's soul in the calm and solitude of the ocean.

The poems of this year do not, however, show much progress in the maturity of the poet's themes. "Nocturnal Stag," a poem quite similar in subject to some of Papatsonis's later works, demonstrates just such a youthful superficiality:

> Like a Revelation the Stag
> appeared before me in the somber
> Moon in the depths of Night.
> The Fountain Spring constantly roars.
> It spreads comfort and pities
> the effort to wash away each annoyance.
> And the constellations spread shapes
> of Triangles, Disks, and Squares;
> Vega, which other nights
> was the only Star
> to shine so brightly, cries all-gold.
> . . . .
> I contemplate feigning the part of St. Eustathius
> whom I read about in Smith's
> fairy tales with his earthly sufferings,
> but my great disobedience
> to Moses's law and my inclinations
> to pleasure which expand my chest
> in yearning hinder me.
>   (1–11; 25–31)

Where such subjects in the later poetry express a state of mind under great suffering, in "Nocturnal Stag" they are aimless, the ramblings of a young poet lost in his awe at a universe peopled by the celestial objects to which he aspires. The poet has not yet the poetic force to make the solitude of the heavens comment effectively on the smallness and insignificance of man.

The first ten years of Papatsonis's career reveal a deeply religious poet whose sense of self is only barely extended beyond simple egotism and patriotic fervor. His verse is simplistic and rhymed for the most part, taking on only at times the free form which is later to become typical of his mature work. Though his themes are similar to those he utilizes throughout his career, they are only tentatively and shallowly explored, and the poet's vocabulary and imagery are restricted to the enthusiasms of an inexperienced young man.

IV   *Poetry: 1920–1929*

Almost half the poems of the twenties were written in the first two years of the decade, most of them (fourteen) appearing in 1921. In these poems one can detect a greater change in the poetry of Papatsonis, for it has become more definitely proselike, having rejected completely the rhyme schemes in use from 1910 to 1919. Further, most of the poems are narrative, a device the poet was to continue in his poems of the thirties and forties. Tales appear of Biblical characters such as Daniel in "Daniel in Fovea Leonum Signata" (1921), Elizabeth in "Elizabeth's Leap" (1921), John the Baptist in "For John the Baptist" (1921), and the Apostles Peter and Paul ("In Memory of Apostle Paul," 1921; "For the Highest on the Second Vespers," 1921; "For the Highest Peter and Paul in Liturgy," 1921; "Peter and Paul, the Highest," 1921)—prominent figures in the poetry of the twenties. The poems progress from an initial objective rendering of a story to subjective reflections on the poet's own spiritual state. In the poet's later religious works a confusion of "I" and "thou" results that permits the poet, like a second Christ, to take on the burdens of his fellowmen—the "we" of his *Ursa Minor*—and to merge into the higher union of God and man. "Elizabeth's Leap" demonstrates the earlier shift in point of view:

> The Virgin Mary traversed steep areas and ascends
>   the mountain to visit Elizabeth,
> There on high in dawn's mountainous freshness nature
>   breathed in relief.

A tent of cloth was spread before the white rural
    home's door
which gave a satisfying shade to the holy hermit
    inhabitants.

. . . .

Today, above all, is the festive memory of Humility's
    hymn
in which the Virgin praised her son and God with
    "my soul increaseth."
If on a lonely wooded hill a church was built,
I would inhabit it with a Priest and the Lord as roof
    and helper
as a permanent eternal memory to the Virgin, who
    ascended the Mount,
drenched by vital peace in perpetual ecstasy within
    a hypnotic Dream.
        (3–6; 21–26)

In 1921 the first of Papatsonis's poems based entirely on classical
Greek themes were introduced. In these works the poet uses
ancient myths and attitudes to refer to the celestial and to comment on the universe of God. In "Rape of the Sabines," 1921,
which exploits the sensuality of the classical era, the liberation of
the sexual act releases man from the physical world on earth and
elevates him to the celestial world of paradise. Classical motifs
reinforcing the poet's religious themes occur in his later poems,
particularly in *Ursa Minor* where classical and contemporary
motifs are combined to glorify the heavens.

In the poetry of the twenties, a world of night and the stars
opens up, and mystical qualities become more manifest. In "Peter
and Paul, the Highest," the poet speaks of his "night of agony,"
and in "Wednesday of the Year" (1921) and "Those Starry Winter
Nights" (1923) he contemplates the night as it casts loose the
varied shapes of the constellations:

What all pure-white or gray spirit, weightless soul
    sits on peaks
and industriously gathers Clouds from North and East
which rise tuftlike and beautiful spreading whiteness
to the sky's expanse? Who but He made Manifest by the
    Mountain,
and these clouds go up in smoke, *tetigit montes et
    montes fumigant.*

> He, after some deliberation, loosed numerous heavenly
> Lions and Dragons
> to mask the firmanent and to sink men in dream.
> ("Wednesday of the Year," 5–11)

The night as a great abyss in which resides "the secret of the
world" (63) recurs in "Passions of Artemis One Saturday" (1923),
a poem in which Papatsonis again uses classical myth to speak
of celestial matters as he relates the "moon of dawn . . . with its
agonizing calmness" (23–25) to Artemis of the "virgin passions" (4).

It was in the twenties, too, that Papatsonis's pantheism, his
insistence on the divine expressing itself through the smallest
particles in the universe to the wholeness of the universe itself,
became a major theme. From the refuge he finds in the beauty
of a rose bush ("Rose Bush," 1925), to his discovery of the essence
of the profound in both that which is good and that which is evil
("The Unlooked-For Theme," 1928), the poet comes to understand God's world as an expression of eternal order and to distinguish it from the chaotic material world of man ("Summer
Tourists Go to Mass in Piraeus," 1929, and "Ode," 1929).

The world of the poems of the twenties is a lush one, lit once
again by a feminine presence ("Beata Beatrix," 1920; "For John
the Baptist," 1921; and "A Monday of the Year," 1921), but a
presence which is extended beyond the person of the Virgin to
that of Beatrice. In this world the poet is made drunk by the
sensuousness of the divine, a sensuousness which is an expression
of the feminine nature of the divine enticing him to regain admit-
tance into the Paradise from which he has been barred ("Happiness's Payment," 1925; "Before the Advent," 1925):

> I feel myself to be a man disgraced,
> walking nightlong and daylong beyond the Paling
> of a Garden lush with fountains and flowers,
> waiting in vain for the Great Gate to open again,
>   and to admit me.
> And I am tired with the remembrance only
> of the evil life I have lived to this day.
> And I am downhearted because I am thwarted now
> when I long to lie down under the foliage of the Shadow
>   of Grace
> ("Before the Advent," 1–18)°

It is in this period that the sun begins to emerge as a central figure in the poetry of Papatsonis, to be merged in the future in *Ursa Minor* with the feminine presence and identified there with the Creator Himself. In "The Stone," 1929, the poet sings of the sun as the power and the center of the universe: "this huge flaming Disk does not cease to be, nevertheless, / the center of all the world around" (5–6).* In "The Ships and Other Things," 1929, it is the sun together with the moon and the stars which it illuminates that form the order of the universe.

The twenties can be considered a critical preparatory period for Papatsonis. An initiate during the second decade of the twentieth century, by the end of the twenties he had introduced in a substantial form the major themes and images which were to preoccupy him through the next forty years. His poetry found its form in the long free-verse lines of the twenties poems, and his glorification of the universe localized itself in the lushness and voluptuousness of the nights in which the poet chose to contemplate the divine and to seek union with God.

V *Poetry: 1930–1940*

Papatsonis's poetry can be viewed as having reached a point in the thirties where the poet was prepared to embark on work of a philosophically more dense and stylistically richer quality. Many of his most deservedly famous poems were composed at this time, including "Outline of Error," 1930; "The Sluggish of Mind," 1931; "The Dependence," 1932; "Adage," 1932; "Encounter," 1933; "Invocation of Images," 1934; "Myth," 1935; "The Old Man's Log of Wood," 1936; "The Inns," 1936; and "The Island," 1939, all of which the poet himself recommended for translation as representative of his most accomplished works.[9]

Papatsonis's language now becomes more abstract and metaphysical; classical and Byzantine Greek as well as Latin phrases are more often interspersed throughout his poems. His choice of modern Greek words has become more elegant, his high demoticism bordering on Katharevusa. The poems have become longer, the lines lengthier, and the free verse more proselike than before.

The themes of the thirties poems concern faith, death, winter, and the order found in the universe. Throughout this period, the poet treats man's lack of faith and urges him to accept Christ without further proof. Faith, and not philosophy, is represented as necessary to one's illumination, for the former by itself is insufficient ("Compilations," 1933). If one requires external signs to believe in God, the poet asserts, the universe itself may serve as the greatest sign of His existence ("The Signs," 1933), though ultimately one must recognize the necessity of accepting the universal order ("Sirens and Necessity," 1936) and find the faith to give oneself to the Creator without question ("The Powerful," 1933):

> Could this expectation of Signs have been given as
>   correspondent to our faith,
> as a strengthening, this thirst for
> Signs—so strong that faith's purpose, day
> or night, is the inquiry: "is it to arrive today or
>   tonight,
> is not the awaited sign coming?" Around us are
> spread the marvels in the likeness of all varied things.
> Always persistent, however, continually
> satisfied "we seek a sign" without which
> is Nothingness; but is it Nothingness? Could it be
>   that without a Sign
> Faith does not exist? In this, no.
>
> ("The Signs," 1–10)

The poet in this period continues to view his age as one in which man, lacking in faith, is concerned solely with material goods. His days, as a result, are as dark as his nights ("The Old Man's Log of Wood," 1935), and he is unprepared for the second coming of the Lamb ("Adventus," 1934),

> Times locked up; locked, tightly locked,
> far from a view of the sky, abandoned
> to winds, storms, snow and gloomy skies.
> Vainly do the cocks crow in the accustomed hour:
> they cannot dissolve the darkness; light does not come,
> bad news arrives. These a muffled-up Old Man
> with a lighted oil lamp receives
> toward noon. Behold the plight
> of the wintry man, indifferent
> to all, fearful only that his log
> might burn down. The hours have proved to be fictitious,
> fictitious the days of the month. Behold, January
> the twenty-first: Agnes the Virginal Martyr (cast

at the age of thirteen into the Gehenna of martyrdom);
    January
the nineteenth, the second Sunday after Epiphany:
the wedding at Cana, Sebastian
and Fabian the Martyrs (they hurled at Sebastian
a shower of arrows, scales on the young man's body).
What's this to us? How can one day now
be distinguished from another? Each is equally locked,
since night no longer stands as a separation between
    them,
since day is ceaselessly being turned into night,
and the only concern we old men have is not the vision
of faith, not Martyrdom with its flames,
but that this log may not burn down once and for all.
                ("The Old Man's Log of Wood") °

The darkness of death permeates the poetry of this period
("Christmas of Tears," 1930; "Song of Transient Things," 1935),
though the poet accepts death as a door that opens upon the
Creator ("Exist," 1932; "Hearth," 1933), and he delights at the
surcease of pain that must come with death ("The Angel Resounds," 1936).

In the thirties the theme of universal order which had begun
to interest Papatsonis in "Summer Tourists Go to Mass in Piraeus,"
1929, becomes more prominent. Contemplating the myriad constellations ("The New Sprouts," 1933; "The Three-Personed Sor-
cerer," 1935), he expresses his wonder at an order in which all
things take on their eternal nature:

            The Sky's picturizations
        are transubstantiated in Persuasion
        concerning divine Order. Correspondingly
        the earthly lose the character
        of matter, of their own matter.
        Rocks, minerals, thick earth,
        sand return only Matter's essence
        with attraction and repulsion
        and an elliptical course,
        the spinning-top of midnight's isolation is made manifest.
                    ("The New Sprouts," 8–17)

The liturgy itself refers him to this order ("Historic Liturgy at the
Cypress Tree," 1938), for it expresses the absolute, a realm, unlike

that of the relative, in which peace and true happiness reside ("The Dependence," 1932).

Such now-familiar themes as the sensuality of nature, the feminine presence, the night as a time of contemplation, and the desire to return to the Garden of Eden are also encountered here, though pantheism is probably the most intensely developed theme of the period. The poet begins here as well to integrate varied elements in his poetry. He describes God through all aspects of nature, finding in the bounty of nature, in the fullness of its vegetation, solace and hope after the pains of life ("The Solace," 1930; "Encounter," 1933; "Sunday," 1933). In "Hibiscus" (1933) and "Myth" (1933), the poet links the sensual ecstasy of nature with night as the time when the beauty of the heavens is made manifest:

> Tremors of dew—what am I saying?—almost a shivering,
> has pierced the Poplar Tree of night; the same rustling
> has been communicated to the depths of our souls;
> together we sang the Hours of Meditation,
> escaping the negations of sleep. The brimming dazzle
> of the Full Moon in the mid-heavens has lit up
> the Poplar Tree of night. Luminous
> Forgiveness, that youthful bird of song,
> flew toward us, came and roosted on the daedalian
> foliage of man. Well then, O Night,
> Night most serene, O most miraculous among
> all other nights, for whom we waited, and you never came—
> behold now, you are here! Continue now
> through the long length of hours; do not disrupt
> the created Equilibrium of the Elements,
> for without it Chaos would come again.
>
> ("Myth") °

The Garden of Eden is described as an intense experience of lushness and voluptuosness which the poet associates with union with God. Lamenting those sins which drove him and his kind from the Garden ("The Expulsed," 1932; "Terminus," 1933; "Triodion," 1934), the poet sings of its beauties and its hope in the belief that man someday will be permitted reentrance ("The Gardener of the Tomb," 1936).

In the poetry of the thirties Papatsonis treats more completely than before man's relation to God and the stupidity and irrationality that prevents him from discovering and receiving Him. In this highly synthesized state of his poetry, the poet has reduced his expression of the dilemma of sin and salvation to its most condensed form, anticipating his most complete expression of it in *Ursa Minor* in which the unregenerate is made to pass through a series of trials before he may once again be considered worthy. He fully developed in the thirties his handling of the major themes of his poetry and prepared himself for his most complete expression of those themes as a total vision of life, an endeavor he was to undertake and finish during the war years of the forties.

VI *Prose: 1927–1944*

Papatsonis's prose in the thirties was related in many ways to his poetry of the same decade as well as to trends which were at that time becoming generally evident in Greek prose writing. As books of travel and works exploring intellectual attitudes were most typical of the prose of the thirties, so did they appear most significant in Papatsonis's own prose. Dimaras observes, in *A History of Modern Greek Literature* that the "Content of the new prose was an epic of the mind, an epic of the soul, adventures of man." [10] These elements are clearly evident in Papatsonis's work.

Most of Papatsonis's important prose, in fact the bulk of his prose, was written during the period of his most prolific poetic output (1933–1944), though individual works were often not collected in book form until a later date. His travel essays on Romania, serialized in *Kathemerine* from July 3, 1939 to December 18, 1939, for example, were not published in book form as *Moldawalachia in Myth* until 1965, while the poet's travel diary from a trip made to Mt. Athos in 1927, *An Exercise on Mt. Athos*—belonging in spirit to the new prose—was not published at all until 1963. A number of critical essays which appeared individually in *Kathemerine* from 1935 to 1940 were collected in 1966 in *The Four Cornered Earth I*; others, published in *Nea Estia* in 1942, were collected along with more recent essays in 1970 in *Friedrich Hölderlin: 1770, 1843, 1970*. The period 1933–1944 was also one in which Papatsonis completed many of his most important translations. Works of T. S. Eliot (1933), Alfred Jarry (1936), James Joyce (1936), Friedrich Hölderlin (1942), and Paul Claudel (1944–1945) were all translated and published during these years.

Papatsonis's prose demonstrates the same preoccupation with

the harmony of the universal order, the same deep faith as his poetry. *An Exercise on Mt. Athos* can be classified, in Dimaras's terms, as "an epic of the soul"; the essays in this work, referred to by the author as "diaries of his soul," are imbued with a trancelike religious feeling inspired by the peace and serenity of monastic life, a life which bestows grace on those who adopt it and which conquers the "death" in life:

I, too, came forth humble and wrapped in my unfurling. Where can I fly in tragic faith's so luminous heights? I, too, came to the window on this night in which one could see the distant shores. And what did I behold! What did I see! Behold, while the supplicating bells rang an enormous Seraphim flying on the left of Giant Athos, flying so that he might engulf the entire celebrating city of angels! On the Giant's peak, the Constellation Cygnus descended from above, a lighted and shining Cross. Behold, the fiery planet, the most powerful lampion! The entire rotunda was a flaming liturgic chandelier. Even the odoriferous sea in its serenity celebrated the bright day which soon would dawn.[11]

The essays on Mt. Athos do not constitute a unified work on faith, nor are they a concerted effort to come to an understanding of the nature and existence of God. Rather, as Papatsonis explains at the end of the work, the essays relate experiences encountered during his five-month stay at the monastery and include humorous and affectionate accounts of the lives of the monks. Composing intermittently, and only as he was affected by his holy surroundings, Papatsonis jotted down quick notes on scraps of paper which he later stuffed, forgotten, into his pockets. Only thirty-five years later on the occasion of the one-thousandth anniversary of the holy mountain were the notes remembered and prepared for publication.

While Papatsonis's stay on Mt. Athos is a work of the soul, his *Moldawalachia in Myth* can be considered "adventures of man." Here the poet describes the scenery of Romania and his experiences along the way; he includes a history of the country and traces the beginnings of its people. A large part of the book is concerned with Bucharest, where the poet resided for thirty-five days, and Costanza, the first city he visited. At times the poet focuses on a work of art, like the statue of Carlos I, the first king of Romania, or a natural wonder such as the Black Sea over which the poet travelled on his way to the country. But however trivial the topic under discussion, these "adventures" always reflect an accumulation of knowledge and a body of faith and feeling which rescue the work from the limitations of its relatively simple format and subject. One still senses the poet's religious awe for nature and his desire to come to terms with God. The monasteries, which recall him to his faith, reveal that the Romanians, like the Greeks, are children of God.

A third group of essays collected in *The Four Cornered Earth I* are of a different nature from either of the two travel books. Taken from the poet's weekly literary column in *Kathemerine*, these essays can best be described, again in Dimaras's terms, as "an epic of the mind." *The Four Cornered Earth I* deals largely with the literary worlds of both Europe and the Americas, the emphasis placed on French and Spanish literature and on the figures of Claudel and Dante. The subjects are not limited to literature, however, but range from a description of the quality of paper in a deluxe French edition and commentary on characteristics of the Cuban people to larger aesthetic questions. The organizing principle of the collection is basically religious in intent—religious in the pantheistic sense as the work of a man who respects the divinity in all things, of one who finds everything in the universe worthy of comment.

In these essays Papatsonis surfaces as a critic. He sees criticism as a work of art standing independent of that which is criticized, the object of scrutiny acting as a catalyst to the critic's self-expression. More concerned with theme than with the formal properties of a work, Papatsonis explores literature in a lyrical fashion, using various works as occasions for lilting displays of feeling. His prose in this work, as a result, is itself a kind of poetry—what Papatsonis himself calls "poetry in prose" [12]—and can be considered an important development in the poet's use of language; for here he extends himself to reach poetry through prose, as he had been trying throughout the thirties to reach prose through poetry.

It was at this time in his career that Papatsonis began to develop an aesthetic theory through numerous essays which he published in a variety of periodicals, including *Semera, Ellenika Phylla, Phrangelio, Ta Nea Grammata,* and *To Trito Mati.* Discussing the nature of the poet himself and of his dependence on society, Papatsonis claims in an essay on Cavafy in *Semera* (1933) that "the greatness an artist achieves is not determined by the artist's violence during a revolution, or indeed even before the revolution occurs, but by the degree of dependence he has on the society in which he lives and on the period in which he lives." [13] Papatsonis continues to explore the same sentiment in later essays, linking his interest in the social determination of a poet to the forms he must ultimately choose in writing his poems in an essay on Ritsos in *Ellenika Phylla* (1936):

I cannot understand how in a period when the metrical molds of former times have fallen aside in poetic perception—and justly, because at no time after the death of Apollo and Dionysius did they represent anything else but the mustiness of the Alexandrians—why they have fallen out also in the perception of the socially undeveloped, in other words of those not on the left. I ask myself why a revolutionary like Ritsos selects these young molds in which to set his revolutionary thoughts. This constitutes an elementary mistake which I attribute to complete lack of aesthetic sense, or to the distortion of aesthetic criterion from a tradition so intense that it suffers from this elementary ignorance or insensibility. [14]

Papatsonis's own aesthetic tastes had by this time, however, crystallized into a form antithetical to the kind of poetry which would serve a social cause. He specifies his aversion to social poetry in his essay on Z. Oikonomos which appeared in 1935 in *Ellenika Phylla*:

[Z. Oikonomos's poetry is good] because with all its inconsistencies and its anachronisms it is the only [poetry] which contains the longed-for seed of life. I have read up to now a great deal of communist poetry, Soviet, and none of it can escape from narrow propaganda, a continuously ugly propaganda. With Oikonomos, however, it is not this way at all. . . . Since indomitable faith enrages [Oikonomos's poems] it is this which gives its nature to great poetry with an abundance of gifts of force and prophecy. I too believe in an analogous faith (all true faiths are analogous); the only difference is that mine does not want the destruction of symbols, for they will be reborn, but wants their blending with the new, which is more physiological. The violent does not initiate, only persuasion does. [15]

Another aspect of Papatsonis's prose (separate in style from the lyric essays and the travel essays) is represented by his critical work *Friedrich Hölderlin: 1770, 1843, 1970*. Though the Hölderlin essays are, like his previous works, imbued with a deep religious feeling, they express more concisely the poet's knowledge of foreign literary history and present a more objective critical approach to the works they analyze. In this work Papatsonis focuses in three separate essays on three poems by Hölderin (included in the book are Papatsonis's own translations of the poems). Using these poems as a point of departure for a comparative study of Hölderlin's work, the author relates him to Schopenhauer and to Nietszche in an effort to indicate analogies between the way each handles subjects of interest both to Greek literature and to the author himself. The kind of criticism which Papatsonis here undertakes reveals the extent of his own wide knowledge of German literature, as well as his ability to draw comparisons between foreign literatures, a talent which does not occur with frequency in modern Greek criticism. He reveals here, more successfully than in *The Four Cornered Earth I*, his ability as a creative artist to function effectively as a critic, applying his own insights as a creator—much as did Eliot, to whom Papatsonis is somewhat indebted in this regard—to the creations of others rather than using the works of others largely as an excuse for self-expression.

VII   *Poetry: 1940–1950*

In the early forties Papatsonis continued to publish his most masterful poems. His "Attic Shapes," 1940; "I Sing the Wrath," 1941; "Divinity of Summer," 1942; "The Bonfires of St. John," 1943; "Harvesting the Fields at Night," 1944; "Crossways," 1944; and *Ursa Minor*, 1944, are among the poems he recommended for translation into English and represent a continuum with the best poems of the thirties. In these pieces Papatsonis continues to comment on the themes which he had most fully developed in the preceding decade. Poems on the beauty and lushness of nature take precedence here, however, as do those on the evening as an ideal time for communion with God. In addition to the prominence of these two themes, the poet stresses the feminine presence through a number of figures from Greek mythology and literature.

Most of the poems on nature written during the forties appear to be different from those which preceded them. Papatsonis ponders, as he has often done before, man's failure to recognize the

wealth he has in nature ("Pastorals," 1940). At times he sings of
the joy that an early morning brings ("Change," 1940) or the
beauty of fields lit by the evening moon ("Harvesting the Fields
at Night," 1944). Elsewhere he sings of the beauties of spring in
simple language ("The First Green of Spring," 1942) or of the
stars, the sea, and nature, but in longer, more complicated verses
("Loud Colors in the Winter," 1946).

Though they appear similar, many of these nature poems differ
significantly from their predecessors, for they have become more
obscure. The poet still revels in the joys of nature, but he now
does so in the more abstract terms of "Attic Shapes," 1940:

> Hail Day, in this your immaterial idea
> of elevation that you shall touch the Moon.
> Hail luminous Crescent; now you dismiss
> the vapors of a morning torpor
> and simultaneously display the Dawn of High Noon
> the virginal caresses of the Graces
> the azure awakening of Sea Nymphs
> and the slow movements of wondrous nakedness.
>
> . . . .
>
> Fleeting and God-sent Blissful Weather stands by her side.
> No matter how brief, this is a moment of eternity,
> utter abolition of the tumescent Night,
> triumphal Songs of Victory, but ready to flower
> beyond the Law, gift of God, negation of Winter.
> (12–19; 40–44) °

In the poems of night the poet increasingly examines the secrets
of the evening, its memories, and its myths ("The Bonfires of St.
John," 1943), and no longer simply revels in the serenity of the
darkened skies or links the night with lack of faith:

> "The night, when birds perch on trees
> and fall asleep, breathes life into myths,"
> the sentry answers. What myths, since an instrument
> of precision is sufficient to show how life
> is interwoven with the stars. And life not in abstraction,
> not as a naked knowledge, a more naked ignorance,
>   but as the most
> miserable endeavor, the most insignificant thought
> of each of us, from the millions of mortals

and the armies, all lumped together, dead for centuries,
all pasturing on the night's dark formations
in the hours when birds are sleeping in the trees.
The night brings us these, and so many other things—
it is impossible for man's song to contain them all.
To some extent the vigilance of our sentry
grasps them here or there and proclaims them,
but for what purpose? We have not the power to deviate
from what the cauldron destines for us in its flames,
and once it writes them down, dear God, they cannot
    be effaced.
Made of blood and fire, its incandescent slate pen
sets its seal upon us while the tempest
of our terrestrial piracy endures. Scarred
with the stamp of fire, we burden ourselves
with the sacrificial fumes of our scorched flesh,
    memories
of our spitted pain that torments us insufferably,
—of that pain which the other night was supposedly
    extinguished,
as it sputtered, by the heartless act that revives it.
          ("The Bonfires of St. John," 10–35) °

It is in these inner secrets and incomplete memories that Papatsonis's poetry of the forties differs most from his earlier work. His
poems, in the process of final refinement, reach their zenith in
their introspection, a quality that characterizes most succinctly
the poetry of this period and which brings it to the peak of its
development in *Ursa Minor*. The turning inward of the poet occurs in his attempt to express the deepest-seated of emotions and
to come to terms with that which transcends the earthly. Without
becoming completely inner-directed, the poet uses his deepening
self-knowledge to employ the themes and images he has developed over his career as comments on his own suffering as
representative of all mankind.

During this period Papatsonis's suffering becomes more intimate
as he himself experiences the horrors of the German occupation
of Greece, losing his mother through suicide. In a world of bar-
baric cruelty, the poet's escape lies in his poetry, and the world
beyond takes on a meaning which inspires far more than admiration. It is, perhaps, because of this more eminent need to escape
that the poetry of this period relies more on the feminine presence,

a theme which proves constant in the forties. More than a divine object of awe, she becomes an active agent whose mission is to guide the poet to the serenity of the eternal order he has sung about since the poetry of his youth.

In *Ursa Minor*, 1944, a work summing up the achievements of the thirties and the early forties, Papatsonis is able to create a union between inner emotions and outer reality. He presents his total vision of the dilemma of existence, coordinating in the fabric of this eight-part work the poetic experiences of thirty years. The metaphysical language and the erotic mysticism which typify his best work are here engaged to describe a mystic journey to God that borrows from Dante's *Commedia* and which is infused with neo-Platonic thought. The work, analyzed in depth in Chapters 3 and 5 represents an epitome in the poet's development which was never to be matched.

The post-1944 poems, on the contrary, show a decline from the poet's previous works. What binds them to the earlier ones in the forties is a deeper introspection, an even greater turning into oneself. The poems of this period are personal, more narrowly religious, like prayers, and less genuinely metaphysical ("Holy Women," 1945). Papatsonis's poetic material is thinner. The images tend to become more restricted and the multiple meanings common to the figures and symbols of *Ursa Minor* tend to appear less frequently and without the same intensity or complexity, as indicated in poems such as "That Which Is Carved in Belief," (1945) and "Reckoning," (1945):

> Alone they came in a certain year,
> came and departed,
> weather forecast
> behind the mountain, and arrived
> at times like siroccos, at times like southwest winds,
> at times like west winds, and each one arrives
> as though for the first time,
> sweeping away the vapors
> of the previous one
> —like the Epiphany, that renews
> all water, seas, harbors,
> clouds, rivers, and suddenly
> the blessed rains come
> and caress our hair, while

doves sketch their flutterings
on the cloudy skies.
("Reckoning," 25–40) ° °

Elsewhere, as in "Choephoroe" (1947), the poet becomes preoccupied with the imminence of death and turns back to some of
his most early themes, devoting himself to the birth of Christ
("The Thread," 1949), the capture of Christ ("Thursday," 1947),
His death ("Where Lies," 1946), and the resurrection ("Resurrec-
tional," 1949; "In the Key of Resurrection," 1946).

VII   *Poetry: 1950–1974*

Since the forties, Papatsonis's poetical output has been minimal.
From 1950 to the present, the poet has published no more than
two dozen poems, fifteen of which were written in the early
fifties. The poems of the fifties do not reveal any common major
themes, but concern a variety of religious experiences. In "Self-
Scrutiny," 1951, Papatsonis concerns himself with Satan, the
cunning one who "has sown his obstacles in shapes strangely /
repulsive" (47–48). In "Monsoon" (1951), "Her Disturbance and
Calmness" (1953), and "The Candle of Easter" (1958), he treats
the season of Christ's Passion, to which he has devoted a number
of poems over his career. Of this group, however, none of the
poems develops beyond a relatively simple expression of the
poet's spiritual state:

> How do you come to me instead of I to you?
> The spot in which I alone placed so much happiness
> did not contain me. Come that we may share it.
> I took the ascent slowly
> during the night with the breeze.
> At times I wake some bird.
> I became warm when the sun appeared.
> Now, near you, how wonderfully
> I rest. If you want me
> I'll remain a bit, sheltered;
> sharing our happiness.
> Come, my sister, that I may kiss you.
>   "Her Disturbance and Calmness," II.1–12)

Several of the poems of this period are of the Virgin to whom
the poet prays for guidance ("For Poor Men," 1953; "Her Dis-

turbance and Calmness"), while occasionally a small church may inspire him to write ("Reverie on the Fifteenth of August," 1959). In some of his best poems, however, one senses a return of his old power. Just such an occasion occurs in the poet's discussion of the divine in nature in "Ode to Aquarius," 1954:

> A crevice of tranquillity, a crevice of meditation
> is this segment of water that
> from the beginning pours out with great impetus
> from the Beloved's bucket, and is poured out
> without cessation; and when the nights
> come star-laden and weighted with gold,
> and when the hermit,
> vigilant in expectations and freed
> from his tensions and his ecstasies,
> feels the sweated blood of his agony
> crowned at last with a certain approach
> of his own to the clues of chaos, when
> filings of gold shower down, during nights
> when the mute, cruel element for one moment at least
> is pierced, then the lone suppliant
> with utter delight clearly hears
> the buckets rattling in their joints,
> the chains that rub and creak
> as they glitter and drip with water,
> the well as it bubbles and overbrims.
> Then he sees the foam sparkling
> and lives now in those lustral waters
> where Zeus himself once delighted.
>   (5–27) *

The eight poems of the poet's latest period (1960–1974), including in 1960 "And to the Greeks Inanity" and in 1963 "Psalms and Encounters", are of moderate length (from fifty to seventy-five lines), the imagery is more philosophical and less visual, and the ideas expressed are drier in tone. The decline in Papatsonis's poetry at this point is evident, for the impulse to create has diminished, no longer generating the richness that pervaded the poems of the thirties and the early forties. In the waning years of his career, the poet retrenches significantly, leaving behind him, however, a legacy spanning two generations in which is included some of modern Greece's most highly cultivated poetry.

IX *Prose 1944–1974*

The prose of the post-thirties period includes a critical work, *National Revolution: Solomos, Calvos* (1970), originally a speech delivered before the Academy of Athens on March 25, 1970, and a collection of essays, *Where There Is a Garden* (1972), similar in style to the lyrical essays in *The Four Cornered Earth I.* The twenty essays of *Where There Is a Garden,* published originally in *Euthyne* in the 1960's, can, like *The Four Cornered Earth I,* be divided into two types of lyrical essay—religious and aesthetic. The subject matter of the essays is again comparable to that of the poems—contemplative, mystic, philosophical—as is the imagery, the lushness of the language, and the intensity of expression. The essays appear to have been composed in a rush of emotion, as if the poet, burdened by an intolerable weight, was struggling to free himself of it. The second essay of the collection, "When the Almond Tree Blooms," is indicative of this aspect of the poet's style:

There the dome's anthill twists and moves the celestial wonders, while here day and night carry a succession of winds, both good winds and the others which shake the very foundations of the sphere. A little farther off the seas, now calm, serene, and enticing, immediately alter without our knowing how. They become agitated, they foam and create plunging waves revealing the thrice-enlarged and thrice-darkened abyss. Even that flaming Sun, that inexorable archer, empties his inexhaustible quiver upon us, then suddenly darkens, hidden by clouds, while the skies burst open in rinsing cataracts. Here a rich plain spreads itself; a little farther off are seen darkened wooded areas and, as one proceeds, mountain noses thrust out as do those of crags and high ice caps on which is performed the holy marriage of absolute desolation during the nights of the full Moon or the small crescent which is always ready and sharpened to reap whatever protrudes and is elated.[16]

In this essay many of the familiar themes of the poetry are encountered: the passing of the years, man's inability to understand the variety of life in its changing seas and landscapes, its darkness and its light, and the poet's own willingness to receive both life and death as necessary parts of the circle that completes the whole. In "Donkey Mill" the poet speaks again of the order and harmony found in the universe and argues against the nonexistence of God, while in "Concerning Weariness and Stupidity" and

"Miscellany and Notes on the Holiday of August 15" he marvels
at all of creation and speaks of whatever he does as a reflection of
his deep faith.

Though other essays in the collection treat literary matters
(dealing with Eliot, Valéry, Claudel, Papadiamandis), they
too are touched by the poet's religious attitudes. His essay
"Even Beyond the End" explains Hellenism in its relation to God.
"Schicksalsverbundenheit," obstensibly on a play by Claudel, explores Claudel's work as a vehicle of faith and hope. Other essays,
such as "The Invulnerable Muse," continue, however, to develop
Papatsonis's aesthetic attitudes. Here the poet probes, as he has
done earlier, the nature of poetry and its relation to man:

The vehicle of Art, either as creator or as a receiver who searches for
it, is Man, the Monad. And man is soul that turns, whether he likes it
or not, in toward himself, and a soul that accepts, assimilates, and
intellectualizes whatever lies outside himself—that is, he communicates
both with the inanimate and the animate world. The trend for a
balance in this function, that constitutes man's nature in life, is also
the creative force of Art as well as the rest of his intellectuality. And
the subversion of this law is equal to death. That's why I'm persuaded
that art is indestructible, the bread of life that is eternal.[17]

Unlike more socially oriented essays of earlier periods, this
essay documents the intensification of the poet's introversion and
a general turning away from any indebtedness to society. It is an
attitude all too typical of Papatsonis's work of the sixties and
seventies in which he isolates himself in a world of private religious experiences.

In the slim volume *National Revolution: Solomos, Calvos,* the
author turns his attentions as a critic to two major Greek poets
and to some extent to classical mythology, first discussing the nine
muses and then focusing on Cleo and Caliope as the respective
muses of history and poetry. Continuing with a consideration of
Calvos as a revealer of history through poetry (a quality Calvos
shares in common with both Solomos and Papatsonis), the book
compares his work to Pindar's in their common use of the Olympian pantheon, and praises Calvos's concern for the Greek landscape and his exaltation of the national revolution. Solomos,
extolled for similar qualities, is especially noted for unifying
his poetry through his use of the central image of the battle

of Missolonghi, a feature which Papatsonis finds expressive of Solomos's abiding concern for the values of the Greek revolution. Even in this work, however, one is met by the same recurring Papatsonian themes of the liberation of the soul, of hope, and faith, themes he links in this study to the works of both Calvos and Solomos, to whom he refers as the "shining lights" of modern Greek poetry.

In spite of the material it covers, *National Revolution: Solomos, Calvos* does not merit the same acclaim as the Hölderlin book, to which, as a work limited to individual poets, it can legitimately be compared. The Solomos-Calvos book was not undertaken as a literary study, but merely as a speech celebrating the day of Greek Independence and, as a result, was composed in the heavily rhetorical or Purist style which is not typical of Papatsonis's best prose writing. The critical ideas he presents are selected for their appropriateness to the occasion of the speech and do not really reflect a thoughtful evaluation of the work of either Calvos or Solomos. As one of the most recent works published by the poet, it is, further, indicative in many respects of the slackening of creative tension that has occurred in the poet's work since the fifties.

Conclusion

Papatsonis's development began in the second and third decades of the twentieth century, a period of pessimism and despair, though his poetry was only lightly touched by those elements. His work, rather, is characteristic of the thirties, in which free verse and surrealism began to appear and a more incorporative, less egocentric form of poetry was being written. In Papatsonis's earlier years he was concerned with making social contact and wanted his poetry to "identify with life and as such to become the common property of all mankind." [18] In spite of this concern, however, he became an early opponent of what he called collective or propaganda poetry "sufficient for dictators and their machinery in order to prescribe the lies of their ideologies." [19] Papatsonis stood apart from his political compatriots as one who had "chosen to frame the Mystery that surrounds man . . . in the symbols of a beautiful, venerable, and ancient myth." [20] Growing more deeply introspective, he began to see man as the vehicle of art, the "soul that turns, whether he likes it or not, in toward himself." [21]

Using the same themes over his career, Papatsonis's poetry gradually matures to its highest expression in the thirties and early forties. Themes of the majesty of God, the destiny of man's soul, the struggle to be worthy, the feminine presence and its intercession on man's behalf, nature as a reflection of the divine, the lives of Christ and the saints, the Greek myths, and faith, hope, and love appear throughout his poetry, though they are most effectively dealt with in the period from 1930 to 1950. Stylistically, his work is a mixture of the mystically erotic and the ecstatic in gradually more complex images of a more and more abstract and metaphysical nature expressing the poet's growing pantheism.

Though his work is characterized by a metrical and rhythmic simplicity and loose structure, it derives some shape from its often simple observation of Catholic ritual, both abstract and literal, and its prosaic and didactic qualities. Often canonically precise and dogmatically naïve in his earlier poems, he developed in the thirties and forties a stylistic refinement of exquisite and intricately devised imagery, the lyricism and complexity of which make him a significant poetic force in modern Greek poetry.

CHAPTER 2

The Feminine Presence: Its Earliest Manifestations

THE most consistent theme in the poetry of Takis Papatsonis, one which he himself has noted as a major force in his work [1] and which has permeated his poetry over a period of sixty years, is that of a feminine spirit which protects, guides, and intercedes for the poet in his search for God. At times she becomes his love to whom the poet dedicates ecstatic melodies, at other times she is a semidivine figure like Dante's Beatrice; she becomes in her purest form a divine creature in both pagan and Christian guises—the Virgin Mary, Artemis, Athena. An amorphous presence, the feminine principle is expressed in some of Papatsonis's best poetry as a fusion of a number of figures, a multifaceted force leading to a submersion of the individual identity in a power larger than itself, and leading utimately to union with God himself.

I The Virgin Mary

"To My Lady and Madonna," 1914, a poem devoted to the Virgin, represents the earliest appearance in Papatsonis's poetry of the feminine presence. The poet's conception of the role of the figure in this poem is a simple one, for he begs her to intercede on his behalf and to reveal to him a "corner of Paradise":

> I seek the throne of
> a peaceful soul to supplicate
> to cry my fate
> and plead
> for my soul's loss
> which is in ruins
>
> . . . .

> You, I implore, show me
> a corner of Paradise.
> (9–14; 27–28)

What is of special interest in this early poem is the use of the adjective *iliostalahte*, or "sundripped," to describe the Virgin, for it ties her role to that of God Himself, an aspect of the function of the feminine presence which is to grow in importance as the poet reaches his most mature expression of this theme.

Through Papatsonis's poems of 1914 and 1915, the Virgin remains a simple forgiving creature. In "My Rosary," 1914, the poet, fondling his "plain white Rosary with its small beads" (1–2), is aware of his unworthiness but is not disturbed:

> the Virgin from above
> forgives and loves me, the good and Blessed one
> . . . .
> the pure Mary with eagerness listens to my prayer.
> (7–8; 12)

The following year, 1915, in "Beyond Snow" the Virgin is still the woman of mercy who will lead the poet from sin. Here the poet's physical love for a woman creates in him an increased sense of shame, which he asks the Virgin to alleviate so that he might love and yet feel free from sin:

> It is for this then, Virgin,
> I prostrate myself today before you:
> enlighten my Confessor
> not to read me some burdensome Canon
> and keep me from speedy Communion.
> Be always near me. I will lose heart
> without you, I repent.
> (76–82)

By 1916 with "Mary of the Afternoon," the Virgin, unidentified in the poem itself, generates into an anonymous erotic force. She becomes "the Mountainous One, dew's Lightning" (6) and appears to the "quiet" man who scales great heights at night to contemplate the mysteries of God. Arising out of the heavens as they open before the poet, she shines more brightly than all else in the evening landscape. Peace and solitude follow her, and man, lost in the ecstasy of such a night, is serene in the knowledge that his love lies before him:

> Until the Stars reveal
> the black night clearly
> and nothing else endures, except the Brilliance
> of the Mountainous One who remains dreamlike
> *Onox, in omnibus vere beata*
> and oh sublime star-lit calmness,
> in which the quiet man is lost in Night's
> sleep, that his love is there.
> (13–20)

The Virgin has now taken on the attributes of Creation itself and has become a figure of erotic attraction. She arrives shielded by darkness, spreading herself in her brilliance before the poet who is lost as if in a dream.

In two poems published in 1919, "The Virgin's Litanies" and "Three Roses," Papatsonis uses the rose as a symbol for the Virgin, a symbol which he borrowed from Dante's *Commedia*:

> Here somewhat leaning, as Mary too is depicted,
> stands a wide many-leafed flower like a divine Heart
> with a sufficiently large stem and several leaves
> (what an unattainable miracle, what holy chills)
> A Rose. But such a personal Rose!
> That in psalms it is justly called "mystic."
>
> *Rosa mystica, ora pro nobis.*
> ("The Virgin's Litanies," 63–69)

Though the figure is still recognizably that of the Virgin, the poet now begins to stress the beauty and frailty of her feminine being, associating her with the loved one whom he longs for. When he addresses the Virgin, he does so in the tones of a suffering lover who wishes his beloved to chastise him:

> Become severe and cold;
> tell me that I am unworthy to examine your litany;
> tell me my recklessness has set me on a dark road;
> tell me that for me suitable is the prayer *Dies Irae.*

The Feminine Presence: Its Earliest Manifestations

> *Regina Sacratissimi Rosarii, ora pro nobis.*
> ("The Virgin's Litanies," 218–222)

So great is the poet's longing for this mystic rose which he cannot attain, that, like a courtly lover, he finds joy merely in being refused entrance into his lady's presence.

As Papatsonis's poetry develops, the Virgin takes on various attributes that link her with mythological figures and attitudes eventually fusing her into a oneness with them. When, for example, Papatsonis refers to the Virgin in 1941 in "Ode on the Death of the Virgin," she is associated with Olympian goddesses as well as with nature. In this poem, the first to sense the death of the Virgin is Pallas Athena, who is seen agitated in her citadel, the other Olympians becoming gradually aware that an event of importance has occurred involving a fellow immortal. Where the death of the Virgin is itself described, the Virgin is pictured as surrounded by and coextensive with nature, all aspects of which mourn her loss:

> Look now Initiates how She is
> hieratically spread on Her altar's white floor
> under the stars within Her majestic
> pillars under the lucid sun.
> Fires assist Her as reddish
> flames fan Her; soot and ashes
> lie in another softness
> and the vigilant-minded flying birds of prey
> never pause, the mighty sentries
> of the Virgin's suspended sleep.
> (34–43)

By 1953 in "For Poor Men" the Virgin is more completely identified with nature. She is referred to as "Mistress of the Sky who adorns / this dome with your deep blue robe . . ." (34–45), which serves as the sky itself. Overseeing the evening firmament, the Virgin is a guider of destinies, one to whom the poet appeals to take an active role in bringing compassion to a world torn by wars and civil strife:

> holy Virgin
> I entice you to quicken the act
> of that hope you inspire in me
> (40–42)

II *Beatrice*

As a symbol of unattainable grace, Beatrice takes the place of
the Virgin in many of Papatsonis's poems. She first appears in
"Beata Beatrix," 1920, accompanying the poet who writes, "I saw
my Beatrice on the road, and all at once the road became a road
of dream. / I walked by her side like a passer-by, and all my soul
blossomed like the Spring" (1–2).* As the poet's lady guide,
Beatrice is more supernatural than earthly, for the road on which
the companions walk becomes "a road of dreams"; her presence
makes the poet's soul blossom and the stars hover about him "like
Guardian angels" (5).* A guide to the mysteries of God, she is
attended by "the flaming sun of Midnight which arose . . . in
splendor" (11).*

Papatsonis's Beatrice is represented in "Beata Beatrix" as a
figure of semidivinity who comes to the poet as one beloved. Their
walk provokes "the interest of all creatures, in love" (17).* As a
figure who eases the transition from the earth to the world beyond, she leads him from the chaos of worldly life to the gifts
offered by heaven:

> We were not disturbed by the encounter of streams
>   or the flight of birds
> nor by the blowing of winds or the vault of fog.
> All was enchantment and gifts from heaven and a deep
>   repose.
>   (21–23) *

In "A Monday of the Year," 1921, Beatrice is more closely associated with Dante's lady:

> With this New Moon, which like a flaming sickle is
>   now setting
> over the distant fields, I saw a Pure White Lady
>   approaching robed like a princess.
> . . . .
> She possessed for me the grace of Daphne when she
> glows green in the flame-flickering darkness
>   (1–2; 6) *

Here the "Pure White Lady" appears as a "flaming sickle" in the
"flame-flickering darkness" and "glows green," taking on the colors
of Dante's Beatrice in *Purgatorio* XXX, 31–33:

> a lady came in view: an olive crown
> wreathed her immaculate veil, her cloak was green
> the colors of live flame played on her gown.[2]

Dressed in white, green, and red, both Beatrices are garbed in the colors of Faith, Hope, and Caritas.

Papatsonis enlarges the Beatrice figure, as he had that of the Virgin, by describing her further in terms of nature's attributes:

> O these entreating marine eyes which, though gazing
>   on mountains,
> recall luminous depths in moments of tranquillity,
>   the only blue ones, moreover,
> in the celestial whiteness, and on waxen hands, and
>   on the virile caresses
> of her linen garment, and on the innumerable pearls
>   around her neck,
> and on the merciless gold of her ring that served to
>   adorn
> a finger on her moonlit hand.
>   ("A Monday of the Year," 14–19) *

Her eyes reflect the luminous depths of the marine world, her face celestial whiteness, and the ring on her hand the moon.

Beatrice approaches the poet as a divine figure: "A flowing radiance spread over her being, a dazzlement invisible in the encounter" ("A Monday of the Year," 3).* Even the air that greets her, as the poet pictures it, is immobilized before her brilliance: "The spirit that blew with a sharp coolness from a fragrant grove of pine trees / stood powerless before her coolness and her dissolving jewels" ("A Monday of the Year," 4–5).* Adorned by the stars ("the dissolving jewels") which disappear with the break of day, she has yet the grace of a beautiful woman; she is compared to the nymph Daphne who was transformed into a laurel rather than submit to the erotic advances of Apollo. A "midnight spirit" (8) * and Empress of the sky, Beatrice is nevertheless still very much a woman, as the final lines of the poem, from Nietzsche's *Thus Spake Zarathustra*, reveal: "Such are Women, in Dressen Suase immer Bitternis ist, Spiel and Gefahr" (19–20,* "And in their sweetness there is always present bitterness, play, and peril").

III *She*

The qualities which characterize the Beatrice figure of "Beata Beatrix" and "A Monday of the Year" are further developed in poems which refer to the feminine presence through the personal pronoun "she." In the first published of these poems, "Passions of Artemis One Saturday," 1923, the "she" is introduced as the moon and identified with the virgin goddess Artemis, a figure to which Papatsonis was to return in *Ursa Minor*: "A moon diseased the light of the stars, / Artemis, I shocked the virgin passions" (3–4). The moon, paling in its brilliance, must give way, however, to the approach of day and the greater strength of the sun's light:

> This suffering and pale moon
> is made even more pale by the omnipresent Sun,
> the pompous one, that he may seem a conqueror
>   (5–7)

The "ever-present" is "the Sun, this pompous one" (8), a masculine force (as indicated in Greek by the masculine gender of the noun as well as by its classical association with Apollo). As the moon is personified by Artemis (and represents, therefore, a feminine concept since Greek words for "moon" exist both in the feminine and neuter genders), the poet finds he has a rival for the favors of his lady:

> How much later in his zenith,
> after a most deep lethargy, like someone foreign to me,
> I confronted him the same day, this one
> to whom I served as a newsbearer in the night,
> and as I preannounced him to the soul of her
> and as I sailed with her in the abyss of night
>   (9–14)

The sun conquers the "she" by day because its light prevents the poet from viewing the object of his desire. But at night in the solitude of darkness, the poet is free to gaze on the moon and to sail ecstatically "with her in the abyss of night."

The feminine presence in this poem is depicted, as in the Virgin and Beatrice poems, both as a sensual and a divine figure. Artemis's rays are stigmata which pierce the poet's heart as God's love, throwing him into a sensual ecstasy of an essentially religious nature:

[54]

> Could those rays which were piercing the leaves of
>   our heart
> have been spears? No, but caresses.
> it was the endless caress which eternity
> dispatched in sensual presence.
>   (17–20)

As has been noted of the other female figures used by Papatsonis, the "she" of "Passions of Artemis One Saturday" is often expressed by the primal elements of nature. She takes on form in a cypress tree:

> This cypress tree some small wind bent
> up toward its top, my evening sister,
> and emitted your shape.
>   (77–79)

Elsewhere she is identified with the earth, which itself takes on yet another aspect of the feminine presence:

> Heavy was the night, like the night after the suffering
> when God under the earth was consecrated.
> But the earth would discharge such a calmness
> when it enclosed the Lord in her mystical bosom,
> this wild feminine affection, on a night like tonight
>   (57–61)

The earth in which Christ was buried is used to link the "feminine wild affection" to a specific form, that of the bosom of the Virgin in which the entombed son was enclosed.

But the "she" of this poem is most commonly expressed as an abstract figure which takes on various aspects:

> Now I will speak of that good maiden.
> In her brilliance she has the stamp of death.
> Imagination is exotic; white is the Sister;
> she has eyes thrice-deep. These eyes and these alone
> kept me company in my wakefulness
> and from their twin source I drew up death,
> gay and beautiful and commanding.
> As for her hair, it is the disaster and loss
> of inconsequential calms.

It was triumphant hair. With goodness
it wrapped me about the road of sleep
in the intoxication of a dream.
(39–50)

The maiden is seen as "exotic imagination" as well as death. She
is white like Beatrice when she first appeared in "A Monday of
the Year," while her eyes are "thrice-deep" and have a "twin
source," relating her, as occurs again in *Ursa Minor*, to both the
trinity and to the double nature of Christ.

This same abstract "she" appears again in 1929 in "If Only." At
first she is described as the goddess of "the all-covering sky / of
autumn" (8–9) who spreads herself across the heavens, giving
new transparency to the sea's pebbles. All existence belongs to
her, and with the assertion of her claim, the poet affirms that all
will become contentment. But this "she" does not remain merely
the goddess of autumn, for soon she takes on attributes of all of
nature:

> But already her voice arrives, from North, South,
> East and West. The horizons all
> reverberate. She comes ubiquitously
> in the essence of the rain or the wind; in the waves'
> froth. The cosmos and man's soul
> are filled by this voice. Let her come.
> Death's time has yet to arrive.
> (22–28)

The "she" figure appears in similar abstract dress in "Bonds,"
1939. There she is referred to as "beautiful Madness" (1) who,
arriving at night, opens for the poet "the boxes of icons" (2), in
which are contained the shapes of the evening heavens. The poet,
abandoning all that has occupied him during the day, rushes to
meet this "Madness" which brings him renewed life. Realizing
that without her all is "barren" (6), he wishes to have her always
by him, though he recognizes that she is unlike any woman he
has known:

> Your affectations are unlike female ones; the thought
>   of satisfaction
> is as foreign to me as the most distant stars;
> you are the source of that gathering

[56]

> which my doubtful existence recommends to the world
> you are the shape and the color of my being, a being
> which without your interposition would remain like
>   disordered
> tiles, ruined, beautiful Madness.
>   (13–19)

The feminine presence here becomes not merely a woman whom
the poet desires sensually, but part of his own being, that which
gives him "shape and color" and order. She is presented as a
mysterious attraction within the poet which draws him toward
the evening heavens, that "Madness" which forces him to abandon
all that he has achieved in the material world and to devote himself to the mysteries of God. "Bonds," in this representation of
the feminine presence, looks forward more completely than any
other of Papatsonis's poems to the culminating shape which this
"force" is to take in "The Attractions," the last and most conclu-
sive poem of *Ursa Minor.*

IV   *Other Mythological Figures*

Mythological personifications of the feminine presence constitute the classical contribution to Papatsonis's preoccupation with
the theme of a blessed female force. The first classical figures to
appear in the poet's work occur in 1921 in "Rape of the Sabines."
In this, one of the most erotic of Papatsonis's poems, the poet
introduces the Sabines, wood nymphs associated with Artemis,
goddess of the forest and the moon:

> Speak to me of the riverine reaches so suddenly
>   populated
> by pure-white radiant bodies scattering their splendor,
> like that of the most brilliant Full Moon at its zenith,
> on the damp shadowy reaches that had never known the
>   sun,
> whose luxurious vegetation had turned into deep darkness.
>   (7–11) °

The "radiant bodies" that here populate the lush vegetation are
"pure white" like Beatrice in "A Monday of the Year" and Artemis
in "Passions of Artemis One Saturday." Like Artemis, these
bodies scatter rays of light which pierce the poet's heart like
stigmata. The rays are referred to later in the poem as those of

the "moon-drenched noon" (22), of a sunless terrain in which moonlit creatures hold sway. Found in "the dark shadowy reaches," the nereids exist in a world metamorphosed by "deep darkness." Though virginal sprites, they are sensuous inhabitants of their surroundings. The poet describes them as completely in touch with nature: "Every tree trunk, every leaf spray, every shrub quivered / with the embrace or the touch of the untouched virgins" (15–16).°

The sensuality of this poem, unlike that of Papatsonis's other poems, is consummated through a physical act. The Romans, travelling on a river through the forest of the nereids, come across the unsuspecting nymphs and despoil them: "the Warriors dropped their lances and their arrows, / completely abandoned to the ecstasy of their divine on-flowing" (23–24).° The poet symbolically represents the sexual act as he describes the soldiers sailing on the stream of Eros which flows toward the female principle. The discarded lances and arrows stress the male organs which were "abandoned" to the ecstasy "of their divine on-flowing." Transporting man from earth to God, the lovemaking of this poem, while carnal in nature, is seen as divine in essence:

> in that astonishing voyage that transported earthly men
> from the nebulae of our ashy earth
> to the purely azure Third Empyrean with its eternal
> splendor in the very heart of the Supreme Sun.
> (38–41) °

Uniting with the feminine presence in her cloistered and shadowy habitat, man rises to "the very heart of the Supreme Sun," to God Himself, the symbols being clearly borrowed from Dante (the Third Empyrean, the Supreme Sun).

The feminine presence that appears in 1930 as the Sibyl in "Christmas Tears" occurs in circumstances fundamentally similar to those of the Sabine poem:

> The Sibyl took fire
> and foretold what is written for me.
> Darkness which was falling from the heights
> spread pressing all around.
> (1–4)

Surrounded by light, this time in the form of fire, the female presence comes again at night and brings the poet news of his salvation. Fulfilling a role similar to that of the other female figures in Papatsonis's work, the Sibyl functions as the poet's guide to God out of the darkness of his life.

Again in 1942 in "Divinity of Summer" the same circumstances prevail in the appearance of Eurydice, yet another classical representative of the feminine presence:

> As night comes and the hours fall
> and all the dazzlement outside
> grows dim,
> this arrogance shall be converted
> toward love, shall be oriented
> toward silence.
>
> Toward Love, and toward the amazement of how,
> imprisoned for centuries
> in darkness, O shadowy Eurydice,
> you have ascended today to shine
> (47–61) ° °

It is at night that man's arrogance turns toward love with the coming of the awaited lady who is Love itself. And it is the feminine figure who out of the darkness brings light as Eurydice herself rose from the darkness of Hades to the light of life.

In 1941 in "I Sing the Wrath," a poem celebrating Greece's resistance to the Italian invasion of World War II through analogies to the Trojan War, Papatsonis introduces a more complicated classical figure, the goddess Athena, as a guide to the Greeks:

> The Archipelago was blackened with the infamies of
>   the abductors,
> and they begged iron loans from the Teutons with which
> to burn down, to turn into ash, the land of their
>   envy, Greece.
> Even so, they were confronted with the spear of Pallas
>   Athena
> shining with serenity, glittering with sovereignty,
> dazzling those eyes that debauchery had fed.

It was the orthodoxy of the Olympians that resolved
the outcome of the battle, as in ancient times, high
in the Olympian palaces. And the immortals scattered
    everywhere,
each with the instruments promised him by the High-
    Thundering God:
the bellows of Aeolos, the wings of Hermes, the trident
of Poseidon, the fire of Hephaestos, the thunderbolt of
    Zeus,
and, above all, the beloved form, the serene
and unperturbed understanding of pure Wisdom,
the panoplied, the flashing, the faultless, the beautiful,
more resplendent than Apollo, with her goatskin shield,
with her luminous and dazzling Spear of Majesty
that blazes in splendor, the Shield of the Virgin,
the Shield which so protects the Sun of Greece
that it may never alter or darken, may never be deprived,
even in the slightest, of its ancient god-born Essence.

(36–56) *

In a manner by now common to his descriptions of the female
presence, the poet presents his female guide through the brilliance
attending her. The enemy is dazzled by the light which this divinity emits, a light glittering with "sovereignty" and blazing
luminously in splendor. A queen like Mary Herself, the goddess
Athena is an untouched virgin. She is received as "pure Wisdom,"
a term reserved in Christian times for God alone. But she is at
the same time a beautiful woman, a "beloved form," although a
"faultless" one "more resplendent than Apollo," the sun itself.
The double function of such a divine force is not only to guide and
protect man, but also to protect that light which she so eloquently
emits, God's wisdom.

V   Conclusion

The feminine presence thus appears in various forms throughout Papatsonis's smaller poems, retaining abstract qualities which
prevent one from completely knowing her. She comes throughout
the poems after the sun has set or appears in dark shadows in the
absence of the sun's light. Throughout she is a virgin, untouched
but desired by the poet, a sensual figure whose beauty is usually
described through the intensity of light that engulfs her. This light
is often the light of the moon, although in an intensity greater than

any light the moon can emit, or, in special events—the appearance of the Virgin Mary or of the goddess Athena—the light of the sun. That she is a divine force is clear from the events that she is seen as capable of controlling: she calms man's soul and fills it with love; she guides him through the heavens and brings him before his Creator. Protecting man from sin, she takes his mind from the mundane affairs of his worldly existence. She is ethereal, unseen but felt, taking often the form of the natural elements and becoming at times like Nature herself.

CHAPTER 3

The Feminine Presence: Ursa Minor

A S the major theme of Papatsonis's poetry, the feminine presence finds its most complete expression in the poet's most significant poetic achievement, the eight-part *Ursa Minor*. It is the Kallisto figure who in this poem presents Papatsonis's most highly developed multivision of that feminine presence, for the poet ties her, not only to divine figures of the pagan and Christian past, but most fruitfully to Dante's Beatrice. Beatrice in Papatsonis's poetry not only suggests the joining of the human and divine in one figure—indicating for the poet her Christ-like nature —but also provides rich literary associations through analogies as a semidivine guide to Dante's Beatrice in the *Commedia*. According to the poet, "This revelation and this philosophy [*Ursa Minor*]" can, in fact, "be very aptly considered to be parallel to Dante's *Commedia*." [1]

I *Kallisto and Beatrice*

The poet's dilemma in *Ursa Minor* lies in the immediate problem of how to escape the living hell of years of war in Greece (the Italian and German invasions of World War II) and how to discover a power which can lift him out of his inferno to some higher sphere where love reigns. It was in this search for escape from the misery and hatred of his temporal existence that Papatsonis kept Dante's Beatrice in mind, for he required a feminine form which could combine sensual feelings together with spiritual ones. He spoke of a woman like Beatrice, loved and desired by the poet, yet unattainable, an intermediary between the poet and the world above, a goddess who could lead him to love.[2]

The twenty-fifth canto of *Paradiso*, on hope, was a particular influence on the poet as he searched for a feminine force to guide him on his journey to God, an influence he acknowledges both in his essay "On *Paradiso*, Canto XXV" (1917) and in a later essay,

"A Triptych from Dante's *Paradiso*" (1963). Regarding hope in *Ursa Minor* itself, he writes: "This force, hope, attracts everything, just as the Pole is the center of the universe; such a magnet and not to consider its existence! This force teaches, enlightens, shines, but it does not burn. If it burns, it burns with the touch of Love. This force calms, reconciles all, discovers the hidden harmonies." [3]

Evidence that Papatsonis had Beatrice specifically in mind during those difficult years is provided by the poet in a letter to the present author dated January 7, 1972: "As far as Dante's *Commedia* is concerned, you can find a similar inspiration proceeding from the vision of a woman-goddess vaguely real but more visibly felt as a divine beneficial power who, in all the crucial moments of my life, has helped me through her miraculous virtue of intervening with and being heard by God. I mean Beatrice." Papatsonis's choice of a guide to lead him through his poem out of the inferno of the war years toward his paradise is thus clearly tied in the poet's own mind to the influence of Dante's Beatrice in the two visionary aspects of the figure: her goddesslike attributes and her beneficence.

In Beatrice, Papatsonis found a figure to whom man could respond sensually in life, but who now belonged among the saints in paradise, an ideal guide in her double aspect as both a loved one and a divine figure. A multiform creature—feminine symbol of beauty and love, both earthly and divine—was necessary to Papatsonis's poem as he indicates in his "Chronicle of Endurance and Suffering": "This marvelous and heroic form, which at the same time held all the properties of women in her love . . . had to be a form beyond and above this world. . . ." [4]

Papatsonis's quest was to discover for his own poem just such a woman, one both beautiful and good, one who could lead the questioning spirit, as Dante was indeed led, from physical love to the love that is God. Associated with the mystery of creation which the love of God permits the poet to glimpse in moments of deep contemplation, she becomes in *Ursa Minor* more than the simple "joy of mystery that took us by the hand to guide us" (20) * in "Beata Beatrix." She is instead "a divine beneficial power . . . with her miraculous virtue of intervening with and being heard by God." In *Ursa Minor* the poet's guide is a central figure, as indicated in the letter noted above; as a release from suffering "the intervention of a lovely creature, sensible and giving courage was a vital need."

Dante's Beatrice becomes in Papatsonis's poem the mythological figure Kallisto. Though, like Beatrice, she stands in the presence of God, no longer a part of the temporal world, she is yet a figure endowed with material form, one of "bones and flesh":

> you who know neither decay
> nor disappearance
> but stand in our midst
> with bones and flesh
> vaulting multihued and smiling
> aborting without hating
> but also without useless sympathies
> all which hung
> accomplices of our dreams
> and all the varied shaped tools
> of our unending hunt
> ("The Quarry," 71–81)

Like Beatrice who rises from sphere to sphere in heaven, the divine Kallisto vaults upward to her source, God. In her corporeal form she represents the putting away of the material aspect of life. She aborts all thoughts and feelings that stood as accomplices to man's dreams: she denies the use of material means to find the true way to God.

Like the youthful and smiling Beatrice, Papatsonis's nymph Kallisto is a young, happy creature, one who, again like Beatrice, died at an early age. Still a young maiden when Zeus deceived her, she was a blossoming woman when she was tranformed into a constellation. She parallels Beatrice as one who is eternal and thus cannot decay, one who will never know "disappearance." She, like Beatrice, is to remain young for all eternity, "vaulting multihued and smiling" ("The Quarry," 75). Her exuberance and joy are those of an innocent wild animal—as indeed she is later described—bounding carefree in the forest.

This exuberance is indicated again in the fourth poem, "The Proclaimed," where the poet describes Kallisto as a force guiding man upward to the heavens:

> a strange meshwork as her absolute
> actuality shouts and laughs

>   dances and resounds
>   (36–38)

The guiding force is that of a woman partaking of the joy and
love of God Who sent her to guide man to Him. Her life-giving
powers are such that without her man must ask:

>   what becomes of all things then
>   and how do they regenerate
>   how might a blade of grass
>   rejuvenate
>   how does a flower bloom again
>   what dead sea spirit
>   will rekindle the iridescences and tempests
>   that pleased us
>   or will set in motion the dolphins' dance
>   to reaccompany our prow's
>   naked joy in the open sea
>   (119–129)

Identified with the joys of God's creation, Kallisto—God's grace—
is responsible for the sprouting blade of grass, the dolphin's dance.
It is Kallisto's presence that provides "our prow's / naked joy in
the open sea." This same joy is expressed in the last poem of
Ursa Minor, "The Attractions," when Kallisto returns in a final
apotheosis to Arcadia, to the dancing of the wood nymphs, arous-
ing "the rapaciousness of Pan" (26) and paling the pearls of the
Pleiades' diadem (28). It is felt again in "The Fates Lead" when
man's soul is set free like a pigeon from its cage to soar upward
to the heavens:

>   all the good fates appeared
>   although so aged
>   to unfasten in the night the pigeon coops
>   simultaneously arousing
>   a brave northerly wind
>   immediately the wild pigeons burst forth
>   playing and revelling crazily
>   vaulting so drunkenly
>   that the night from
>   mellifluousness turned at once
>   into a windy threshing-floor. . . .
>   (95–105)

Here is expressed the same joy, the ecstasy of Dante's release from the constriction of purgatory when he could soar at immeasurable speed up toward the Empyrean (*Paradiso* I).

II   *Kallisto as Guide*

Just as Beatrice awakens Dante to the world of the spirit when she addresses him from the chariot that bears her (*Purgatorio* XXX), so does Kallisto in a parallel manner awaken her poet from the lethargy of his material life. Not until the appearance of Kallisto does the poet's life gain new meaning:

> until you trumpeted
> your awakening triumph
> the end and our resurrection
>
> until you reversed
> our life and its values
> until namely you blew to us
> the spirit of life and of prudence
> because whatever we stood for you taught us
> to be life in name only
>   ("The Quarry," 53–61)

The poet is alerted by Kallisto, who intervenes physically to waken him from his stupor. She trumpets "the end and our resurrection" and blows "the spirit of life and of prudence" as a sensual agent reviving the poet's senses. The acceptance and realization of Kallisto, first as living flesh and then as spiritual awakening, represent new life, a higher form of life, breathed into the poet's soul. In "The Quarry" she guides to

> wake us
> yield us courage
> and "the door wide-open"
> not at all "closed"
> far from our thousand fears
> call to us from beyond
> the great open-air
> not peace but the rallying-cry
> of approach for battle
> whoever wins
>   (91–101)

Kallisto has arrived at a time of need to help guide the poet to salvation, for though he had sought it for himself in various ways, none were satisfactory. He now calls on Kallisto to wake him, to give him courage and knowledge so that he may find the way. He asks that the doors of heaven be kept open to him, for through her guidance he will struggle toward heaven. He asks to be led "from beyond the great open-air" upward into heaven so that he may begin his trip to paradise. Like Dante, the poet realizes that the ascent to heaven is a difficult one filled with struggle, even with a guide to lead the way. He asks only to be shown the right path which has been lost to him, realizing that he must prove himself worthy of the open doors of heaven. Papatsonis, like Dante, does not seek Kallisto as one who will end his strife on earth for the peace of oblivion, but rather as she who will show him the path to God so that he can struggle toward Him.

Kallisto is not specifically referred to as a guide, however, until the fourth poem of *Ursa Minor*, "The Proclaimed," where the "angelic visitor . . . appears to guide us" (11–13). In the same poem, Kallisto's function as a guide is made clear:

> she is largely the donor of wealth in life
> the bestower of the straight way
> she greatly lulls the turbulent
> and alleviates the irascible
>   (79–82)

The "donor of wealth in life," Kallisto provides man with the faith necessary to attempt the path to God. She is called "the bestower of the straight way," for it as she who shows the "True Way" to God. She is the one who guides man to peace of mind, who makes sweet all that is irritable in man divorced from his Creator.

In the final poem, "The Attractions," Kallisto appears again as both the guide of man and the celestial host who guides the course of the planets and the stars (19–21). In a function beyond even that of Beatrice, she gives "a purpose / to random roads" (46–47), and directs "the cosmic dances" (48). She acts, like the pole star at the tip of Ursa Minor, as a fixed point of reference in the heavens.

Likened to the polar star, Kallisto is, according to Papatsonis's "Chronicle of Endurance and Suffering," "like the Pole, the center of the universe. . . ." A divine guide ever present, Kallisto in her theological function behaves as does the star: she "enlightens, shines," but "does not burn." Her power is such, the poet explains, that since "only with the starry harmonious attractions of the universe could she be likened, my mind was directed to the polar star." [5] The polar star, he goes on to specify in a letter to this author dated September 5, 1971, becomes the referent for Kallisto because as the last star of Ursa Minor "which is always stable, it is the *only* star in the northern celestial hemisphere which never changes its position, showing the North permanently and serving for many centuries as a guide to seamen in times when the compass was not yet invented. . . ." Like Beatrice, Kallisto's main function is thus to be a guide to man, and it is to him that she makes available the heaven of God with all its wealth. Like Beatrice, Kallisto is a "guide to God" who turns the poet's "thoughts along a happier course" (*Paradiso* XVIII, 4–5). It is Kallisto who directs toward him "the caresses of the fixed stars" (51–52), the love that he experiences from gazing into the firmament of God filled with all His planets and stars.

Papatsonis's use of Kallisto in *Ursa Minor* has much in common not only with Dante's thematic use of the Beatrice figure, but also with the latter's symbolic treatment of the figure. Kallisto parallels Beatrice in that she has not been created by the poet as a fiction of his poem. She exists both inside and outside the poem, coming to the poet with a history, an experience which preexists the composition of *Ursa Minor*. Thus, like Beatrice, she has for the poet a being quite apart from the poem. As a martyred innocent in the classical myth, she comes to embody in the poem the same values represented by Beatrice: she is the image of hope in a time of despair, of faith in spite of her suffering, and ultimately of all-encompassing love. Both Kallisto and Beatrice function as expansive symbols in their respective poems, particularly in their association with beauty and light and the increasing brilliance of those properties as man rises nearer to God.

As in the opening of the *Inferno*, the dedicatory poem of *Ursa Minor* is bathed in darkness. Man's vision is blurred, for he has strayed from the path of God and has immersed himself in the blood of his fellowmen. Papatsonis's inferno is revealed in this poem as memories of the suffering and hell of the Second World War, memories which separate man from the lovely creature who waits to unite him with his Creator:

[68]

and each breath behind the rails
in the dampness of the garden at midnight
along with all its scents at midnight
the warmth so tepidly blown to me
is the exaltation of a single perfect
blood clot thickened in the darkness
("A Fearless Woman Dressed in
Many Carnations," 99–104)

Papatsonis refers to darkness three times in these five lines. All the poet can feel is the agony of the war that engulfs him. Blood and suffering have clouded his vision and he can no longer see the beauty of God to which the woman before him wishes to lead his soul. It is because of the agony of the war that

the spring stars
and the whole bulging moon
for so many years now reveal
dangling drops of heavenly tears
for this the sharpness of our vision
has dulled so greatly
("A Fearless Woman Dressed in
Many Carnations," 117–122)

It is because of his bitter experiences that man can no longer perceive the beauty of creation or consider his relation to God. It is because of these experiences that Kallisto remains in man's memory as a red icon, an image bloodstained by man's burdens.

In the second poem of *Ursa Minor*, "The Quarry," the poet welcomes Kallisto in his time of need. The poet recognizes Kallisto as the "flaming presence" (63) and the "tangible star" (64). The emphasis of "The Quarry" is on light, in contrast to the previous poem which was plunged in darkness. With the coming of Kallisto there is light, heavenly light. Whereas in the previous poem Kallisto was pictured as frightening (as an icon of suffering to intercede between man and God), here she is seen as "more beautiful than icons," her beauty being affirmed in her brightness. She is compared to objects found in heaven, to its stars and its clouds, in her heavenly aspect.

In the third poem, "Faith and Hope," Kallisto in the guise of the polar star becomes still brighter than before:

evening came with its own honey tones
with its own crispness and flux
the first indistinguishable star approached
pride of Arcturus nose of the celestial paper-kite
and bore everything from us without prudence
all that suffering the lingering hours
the crippled times had slowly spun whatever
absence lack privation had pictured black
how at once everything dissolved in your half-darkened
evening and half-latent entrance
as you arrived with so many gifts
(12–22)

All is made clear to man with the coming of the evening and the first star Polaris. Found at the tip of the little dipper, the Ursa Minor constellation, the Polaris is referred to as the precursor of comprehension, for the first star is the messenger of God's light and wisdom; it is the bearer of celestial news and no ordinary star.

Kallisto is here present in the constellation Ursa Minor. She is the celestial paper-kite. Her brightness is that of a star, to which she is likened in the previous poem ("The Quarry," 62–70), but one star in particular—the polar star that guides men to their destination. More brilliant than usual—for the poet calls her in her intensity "pride of Arcturus," an extremely bright star—her light arrives to find the world still in darkness; it is her light which must show man the way to God and His love which will completely infuse the world with light. But the presence of Kallisto as light erases from the darkness of memory all the suffering and the pain of man's earthly life. Thus, as the intensity of Kallisto's light increases from a dulled vision to a "tangible star," to the "pride of Arcturus," the world of Papatsonis becomes filled with greater serenity. The poet's memories of war dissolve in the darkness of the night that is increasingly being filled with light.

In the fourth poem, "The Proclaimed," Kallisto is seen as a "lightning presence which moves and resurrects all things" (23–24). She arrives with great speed, unexpectedly, full of intense light and with the power of healing regeneration. Kallisto is here miraculous, a quality Dante notes in Beatrice in Canto XVIII of *Paradiso*: "seeing that Miracle surpass the mark/of former beauty . . ." (61–62). In "The Proclaimed," where the poet is

[70]

troubled by a final question concerning Kallisto, she is again described in images of light:

> IF EVER SHE LEAVES
> if ever the sling in its giddiness
> whirls so as to disconnect
> from our stellar system
> this red-hot counterweight of the sun
>
> if the cataract of the empyrean's blaze
> evades our
> orbit's course
> (111–118)

Kallisto is seen here as a sling which keeps the stellar system operating within its given rhythm. If that force should be disrupted, chaos would result, just as man, if deserted by his guide, would be destroyed. She is likened to a "red-hot counterweight of the sun" and to a "cataract of the empyrean's blaze," having so grown in intensity as to be considered comparable to the highest forms of celestial brightness.

In the seventh poem of *Ursa Minor*, the poet describes the universe as revolving about this divine guide Kallisto, the source of life, for she is part of the Creator upon Whom all depends:

> All things revolve around
> life's source
> all throb and vibrate
> around her glitter
> (1–4)

All is full of life in the presence of Kallisto who, with her radiance, gives life to all creation. Kallisto is seen, further, as the heart of the immense being that is the universe, as the organ responsible for its functioning. Here Kallisto in her glitter expresses not only something miraculous and divine, but the very essence of life as the life-giving female principle.

Throughout *Ursa Minor*, Kallisto grows in brightness from a mere shining presence able to light the darkness of the world to an intense form of heavenly light infused with the very "glitter" of life's source. In "The Attractions," she continues to increase in light and beauty, being received as a Christ-like figure in all the splendor of a second coming in the noon of a summer day. She is depicted, like the sun, as weaving herself among the signs of the zodiac, and is described as "directress of the stars / helmsman of the sun which binds us" (129–130). In her final revelation she is likened to God Himself:

> for this revelation
> of the ethereal crimson we exhausted
> one long century
> all our hours' agonies
> at the observatory of such yearning
> > ("The Attractions," 121–125)

The "ethereal crimson," the royalty of God's light, is reserved for Kallisto's final transformation from her initial form, in the dedication, as the dark and fearsome bloodstained Erinys. The darkness of Kallisto's Christ-like bloody wounds is redeemed in the light of the "ethereal crimson." Like Beatrice, whose final appearance is bathed in the divine brilliance of the heavenly Rose in which sit all of God's elect, Kallisto here achieves her fullest expression as the feminine presence.

III   *Kallisto and Christ*

Kallisto's parallels to Beatrice become most apparent in their common analogies to the divine figures Christ, God, and the Virgin Mary. Kallisto's Christ-like nature is most clearly illuminated in her first appearance in *Ursa Minor* in the fifth poem, "Before a Journey." This appearance occurs, as does Beatrice's first appearance in the *Commedia* in *Purgatorio* XXX, at the center of the work (excluding the dedicatory poem which serves as an introduction to the whole work, much as the first canto of the *Inferno* serves to introduce the *Commedia*). In both cases a processional attends the Beatrice figure whose introduction is treated as an analogue to the second coming of Christ.

"Before a Journey" presents the dawn following a night of contemplation and shows the poet prepared to face the journey of a new day with fresh insight. Beginning with a reference to the night of the preceding poem in which the poet loses himself to his spirit, the night is described as a time during which the poet's doubts are destroyed:

> All the virgin gold's numerous illuminations
> burnt and dissolved
> this brief night
> the roving one also lent relief
> which this evening was revealed more inclined
> to alchemy more bountiful
> and industrious
> now the ashes have erupted
> and dispersed they tell us
> that perhaps day is dawning while within them
> they preserve alive
> a belated spark
> it too will be quenched by our poking
> the spears will thunder
> on copper panoplies
> the naked nymphs will shake their disoriented
> sistrums when the chariot
> and great war carriages emerge
> to carry us along
> that we may journey once again
> with the all-devouring
> our rich radiant negro
> bearing his wealth as merchandise
> (1–23)

The processional itself can, in one respect, be seen as an extended metaphor of the coming of the new day. The poet refers in line 1 to the "virgin Gold's numerous illuminations," the stars that adorn the sky before the sun has risen, and which seem now to be losing their light at the approach of day. The sky itself seems to have been more inclined to alchemy, the beauty of the evening being magical as well as joyful, for the poet has made contact with the divine nymph Kallisto. The ashes, the early grayness of dawn (reflecting to some extent the tension of the previous night), have now flared up and tell of the coming dawn. But even as the first light of day breaks, as the ashes of day spread themselves throughout the heavens, the poet perceives a belated spark. These final colors of dawn which the ashes harbor will, the poet says, be put out with our poking. The last remnants of the consuming experience are but the ashes of an exhausted fire.

As the poet introduces the new day's sun, the imagery shifts from the domestic to the mythological. The sun enters as an ancient warrior on a golden chariot and is accompanied by naked nymphs shaking their rattles in a procession of armed carriages. The image recalls Aurora ushering in the sun attended by the hours in spectacular panoply. We, too, says the poet, will be taken up by the naked nymphs, the hours. We will journey once again with the "all-devouring one," the shiny negro, the sun which burns and consumes the day. The sun's power of burning is objectified in the blackened skin of the negro who, like an ancient slave, is loaded down with goods. In this instance, however, the dark-skinned man is carrying his own riches, those the sun carries to the day.

Just as Dante's Beatrice is attended by the rising sun in the thirtieth canto of *Purgatorio*, so is Kallisto in her procession, the rising sun being a medieval image of the coming of Christ. Dawn occurs here, for the first time in *Ursa Minor*, only after the poet is able to look into the heavens and feel the presence of his lady. She is the attraction who is to pull him out of the sphere of the earth upward to the fixed stars where she reigns as the constellation of the Small Bear guiding men to their salvation. The sun arrives after a special evening, for the moon, the wandering one, is "more inclined to alchemy" ("Before a Journey," 6). All of heaven seems to have been aware of the imminence of a great coming, presaging it in the unusual brilliance of the preceding evening in which "all the virgin gold's numerous illuminations / burnt and dissolved" ("Before a Journey,"1–2).

The sun is described as "all-devouring," an image pointed out again in the seventh poem, "The Petrified Insect," where "the voracious noons" appear, referring to the height of day when the sun is directly overhead:

> the voracious noons
> when with His gigantic torch
> God sets fire to all things
> the gaping noons
> consuming without being consumed
> kindled and kindling
> (163–168)

It is during the voracious, all-devouring noons that everything in the universe is caught in the flames of a fire lighted by God

Himself. The middle of the day when the sun is at its height is the time when God's presence is most apparent, and when man feels as if the whole universe is on fire. These noons are miraculous ones, for they can consume without being consumed, like the holy fires of Yeats's "Byzantium." They are the noons of God, the time when Christ is traditionally said to have been crucified, and when, taken into God's presence, we are consumed. These voracious noons never exhaust themselves of their fire, but eternally burn with the unquenchable fire of God, for they are noons kindled by God's gigantic torch, the sun, and which in turn kindle men with the fire of God, His presence. It is this voracious "one" that rises in early dawn in "Before a Journey."

Kallisto's divinity and her associations with Christ are also evident in "The Petrified Insect," where Papatsonis refers to his travellers as three teams: "we journey together / we are three complements" (186–187). The first of the three is Kallisto, the "meteor" fallen off the furnace of the sun; she is the constellation Ursa Minor with its seven stars, part of the light of the sun sent to the poet to guide him to heaven. The second part of the triad appears only when man accepts the spiritual life offered him by his guide; it is the sun, representative of God, which, like Kallisto who shares its substance, is despotic. The third "complement" is represented by the poet himself, man tied to the chariot of "your double might." The chariot is that of the sun and Kallisto who appear, like Dante's griffon, as the two aspects of Christ: the sun as the divine and the nymph as the human.

In lines 19–21 of "The Attractions," Kallisto is herself treated as an image of the sun which, as indicated, refers to God:

> she takes the Twins as talisman
> ignoring the neighboring beasts
> maintaining the destined road

Here Kallisto moves along the path of the sun through the sign of Gemini. She is travelling "the destined road," a reference to what is to come—the return of the martyred nymph to the homeland out of which she was driven, the second coming of Kallisto to Arcadia:

> the five-pointed snowy peaks
> in full summer will receive her

[75]

the Dryads opened for her
all asylums in the Peloponnesus
the rapaciousness of Pan was aroused
Zeus's gold work blazed
the pearls on the Pleiades' diadem
paled
the world's astrologers
were cast into disarray
even the most arrogant Artemis
first discerned the whips
of jealousy hearing enthroned
in her region Kallisto
so marvelous and full of flowers
(22–36)

The earth's astrologers, cast into disarray at the intensity of her
light (that of the polar star), are like those who were thrown into
turmoil at Christ's birth by the brilliance of the star over Beth-
lehem. Arriving "full of flowers," Kallisto is like Beatrice in *Purgatorio* XXX stepping out of the Griffon-pulled chariot, wreathed
in flowers, the flowers serving as a symbol, not only of the stars,
but of the soul as well.

Kallisto's coming is likened also to the second coming of Christ
as Papatsonis himself seems to suggest in a letter dated September
5, 1971, explaining "the five-pointed snowy peaks" ("The Attractions," 22): "The image refers to a majestic vision of Mount
Taygetos in the Peloponnesus, one of the highest mountains in
Greece, with five peaks, and covered with snow during the whole
year. It localizes the final apotheosis, where the nymph Kallisto
(Ursa Minor) is glorified in a triumph. This is a symbol of the
final victory, a double one: the victorious end of the Second World
War and the triumph of a great, passionate love."

The return of Kallisto as described in "The Attractions" finds a
further analogue in a passage from the *Paradiso* where Dante, in
the sphere of the fixed stars, sees a vision of Christ:

As Trivia in the full moon's sweet serene
smiles on high among the eternal nymphs
whose light paints every part of Heaven's scene:

I saw, above a thousand thousand lights,
one sun that lit them all, as our own Sun
lights all the bodies we see in Heaven's heights;

and through that living light I saw revealed
the Radiant Substance, blazing forth so bright
my vision dazzled and my senses reeled.
                    (XXIII.26–33)

Here one finds the same dazzling light that occurred at the coming of Kallisto. In the *Paradiso* Trivia (Artemis, the moon) smiles and heaven (the stars) shines in joyful expectation as the world is infused with so much light that Dante is dazzled and his senses reel. Through this dazzling light Dante sees revealed "the Radiant Substance" (Christ), just as, through the brilliance of her light, the poet of *Ursa Minor* discovers Kallisto "so marvelous and full of flowers" ("The Attractions," 36), Kallisto of the "ethereal crimson" (122).

IV   *Kallisto and God*

Like Dante, who describes his Beatrice not only in terms of Christ but also in terms of the sun and God, Papatsonis extends the analogies between Kallisto and Christ through God-like attributes which he ascribes to her. The images of the sun, love, God, and Kallisto are fused, for example, into a complex of images in lines 37–60 of "The Attractions" in which it becomes clear that Papatsonis sees Christ, Kallisto, and God as related phenomena:

> you are the great magnet of the world
> your yoked beams
> invite us irrevocably
> to your seductive net crafted
> with golden threads
> your Dancers arabesque around you
> while you modestly
> nurture all the suns
> perpetuate their flames
> give purpose
> to random roads
> you conduct the cosmic dances
> when goodness overcomes you
> you direct toward us
> the caresses of the fixed stars
> when outraged you nail
> the constellations' fearful patterns
> on the abyss eternal impediments

reaping their royal silence
you extend the icebergs
and reflect them in your heaven
you clothe in opulent snowy fur
the animals of the arctic stretch

Love and the sun are identified with Kallisto as "the great magnet of the world." The great magnet is the attractions, the stars of Ursa Minor which draw us toward the heavens and union with the Creator. The great magnet can also be seen as the sun around which the earth and all the planets revolve. It is a sun of twin lights like the two ends of a magnet, but also like the twin eyes of Kallisto and of Aphrodite, goddess of love, which attract us toward the heavens. It is these eyes that attract us toward the golden rays of the sun and catch us in their net ("The Attractions," 38–41) which, like God in the poem, has a tripartite nature. The sun as the ruler of the universe is ensconced as a great emperor around whom dancers twirl. The dancers are the planets revolving around a sun which feeds all the other suns (stars) that hurl about the universe. But in the same instance the sun is Kallisto-Aphrodite, who pulls us into her net of love while her handmaidens encircle her in joy.

It is the sun which shows the direction, and thus gives purpose, to random roads. It is the sun which keeps the universe in balance, and which maintains the eternal operation of the heavens. The sun, like the Ursa Minor with its polar star, is a guide and director of all the other stars. The sun, like the Ursa Minor (a fixed constellation located above the North Pole), "balances" the other stars. At the center of the universe, it finds disposed about itself, as does the Ursa Minor, all other planets and stars.

The sun is the initiator of all things. It is the sun which, moved by goodness, may direct upon us the caresses of the heavens with all its stars. It is the sun which fills the sky with the bestial shapes of the constellations when it is angered. The sun's anger or goodness depends, in one sense, upon the state of our acceptance of God's love. With love the universe is a kind place engulfed in the embrace of the stars; without it the heavens constitute a gaping abyss filled with monstrous shapes.

As the poet develops the image of the powerful sun that directs everything in the universe, it gradually becomes more and more clear that the sun is the power behind the universe itself, God.

[78]

The "you" which first described love and then the sun is God Who provides for the icebergs and the polar animals (both associated with the North Pole over which the Ursa Minor is to be found). In the context of an exploration of the heavens of the Creator, the reflected icebergs become the clouds which move serenely across the heavens, and the polar animals refer to the constellation of the bears after which the work is named.

V *Kallisto and the Virgin*

In addition to the parallels between Kallisto and Beatrice as figures likened to Christ and God, qualities of the Virgin Mary are contained in both female guides. As Ernest Beaumont notes in *The Theme of Beatrice in the Plays of Claudel*: "Mary is the prime mover in the *Commedia,* and Beatrice, her emissary, is in a sense at one with her and her virginity and her maternity, for to Dante she is both virgin and mother; she is pure, freely reflecting God, and she is a mother in that she watches over him, guides his steps and is above all, the begetter of his beatitude, the bearer of love." [6]

The same parallelism between the Virgin Mary and the lady guide of the poet occurs in *Ursa Minor* through Kallisto's association with Artemis, the classical virgin goddess, as well as through Papatsonis's expressed desire to create for his poem a woman above all women, one who, like Mary, embodies all aspects of womanhood: "My mind then decided that this marvelous and heroic form, which at the same time held all the properties of women in her love—of the Mother, of the Sister, of the Loved one—had to be a form out and above this world, a divine form belonging to eternity, an idea of Goodness and Beauty and of difficult Need." [7]

As a result of the close relation between the Virgin and the figure the poet designed for his poem, Kallisto often functions as a referent to Mary. In "The Petrified Insect," for example, the poet speaks of sitting at the feet of "your sovereign," referring to Kallisto:

> when seated on a stool
> before your sovereign feet
> we measure
> and remeasure
> the uncountable

the alternating hours
on your apron's jasmines
(110–116)

The image here is that of a subject bowed before the feet of a queen. In this prone condition he counts the infinite and eternal hours, time that lies in the lap of this queen as the jasmines of her apron. Within each hour of eternity is to be found the presence of the soul and God. This image also suggests the mother before whom her children sit bowed in reverence, while in her lap lies the grace they seek. With its emphasis on the mother, the queen, the bearer of grace, the image befits the Mother of God herself.

In a later passage in the same poem the reference to the Virgin Mary is made clearer:

often with the purity
of your white flowering
occasionally with the insatiable yearning
of the erect lily
which vainly annunciates
    her fulfillment
(142–147)

In this passage and in the lines preceding it, the poet has been counting the passing of time. Man on earth, as he yearns for his beloved, counts and recounts the hours of her absence. He measures time by the flash of God's caress stretching across the heavens, or by the purity of the white jasmine in the apron of the soul. Sometimes, when he looks upon God's eternity, he yearns to announce the fulfillment of the soul. Such a yearning is expressed by the lily which "annunciates / her fulfillment," a lily like that from God, brought by Gabriel to Mary to announce the birth of His son, Christ. The purity "of your white flowering" associates the sign of the imminence of Christ with the virginity of Her who was to bear Him. Kallisto's role through analogy to the Mother of God Herself is here expanded beyond that of a mere mother or queen to one who stands at the very source of the birth of love.

VI *The Myth of Kallisto*

The feminine presence in Papatsonis's *Ursa Minor* is expressed in classical as well as Christian parallels, for the poet wished to represent in his lady the spirit of his own people's struggle against oppression, to create one who would function as an integral part of the imaginative world of the Greek nation. Personalizing the mythological figure Kallisto to his own use, Papatsonis found in her a reflection not only of his native Peloponnesus (for according to Ovid's *Metamorphoses* II.410–411, Kallisto was herself from Arcadia), but a personification of suffering as experienced by all Greeks during the war. An image of patient endurance, Kallisto kept her faith during her fifteen years of exile, in spite of the painful nature of her trial which Ovid describes in his *Metamorphoses*:

So saying, she Hera caught her by the hair full in front and flung her face-foremost to the ground. And when the girl stretched out her arms in prayer for mercy, her arms began to grow rough with black shaggy hair; her hands changed into feet tipped with sharp claws; and her lips, which but now Jove had praised, were changed to broad, ugly jaws; and, that she might not move him with entreating prayers, her power of speech was taken from her, and only a harsh, terrifying growl came hoarsly from her throat. Still her human feeling remained, though she was now a bear; with constant moanings she shows her grief, stretches up such hands as are left her to the heavens, and though she cannot speak, still feels the ingratitude of Jove. . . . How often was she driven over the rocky ways by the baying of hounds and, huntress though she was, fled in affright before the hunters!
(II,. 476–492) [8]

Kallisto, the innocent and beautiful maiden, is turned into a hairy beast, her peaceful existence in the virgin goddess's forest to be supplanted now by roaming alone along those same paths as a hunted beast, the victim of forces more powerful than herself, forces that invaded her home and turned it from a sanctuary to a living hell. But her suffering was not fruitless. With Zeus's intervention, she was transposed to a finer world than she had known before.

As an image of faith rewarded and hope fulfilled, Kallisto provided Papatsonis with a model to cling to in the terrors of a war in which his native land was invaded by hostile German forces. She who had risen above the agony of her earthly existence to a serene world shining in her victory, into the world of the polar star and paradise, was the envy not only of mortals, but of

[81]

the other gods as well. Kallisto stood, as Ovid describes her, "at the very peak of heaven" (*Metamorphoses* II.517), a realm to which the poet reached out in the brutalized world of his poem as that place where "love reigns" ("The Attractions," 132). A "personalized wartime divinity," as Papatsonis describes her in the essay "Chronicle of Endurance and Suffering," Kallisto provided a native source through which to express the social chaos of the poet's own times: "I thus easily in this way," he says, "entered the regions of the beautiful myth of the bride Kallisto and her love with Zeus himself, and the source of this divine love, the most Greek Arcadia." [9]

VII   *Kallisto and Artemis*

Quite apart from her own natural attributes, the beautiful Kallisto was a figure confused in mythology with the goddess Artemis as Pausanias's relation of the myth in *Hellasos Periegesis* VIII.35.8 suggests. John Cuthbert Lawson in his *Modern Greek Folklore and Ancient Greek Religion*, speaking about the divinity of Artemis in modern-day Greece, indicates the linguistic basis for the confusion of the two figures: "In Aetolia I was fortunate enough to hear an actual name assigned, *e kyra kalo*, 'the lady beautiful,' where the shift of the accent in *kalo* as compared with the adjective *kalos* is natural to the formation of a proper name, and the feminine termination in *o*, almost obsolete now, argues an early origin. The name therefore in its present form may have come down unchanged from classical times; but, whatever its age, we may at least hear in it an echo of the ancient cult-title of Artemis, *Kalliste*, "most beautiful." [10]

Artemis was a triple moon goddess who fed her hinds on trefoil, a symbol of the trinity. She has been referred to as both Triformis and Trigenia, as Luna in her heavenly form, Artemis on earth, and Hecate in Hell. Her tripartite nature is reflected in the triple Dantean theme of *Ursa Minor*—faith, hope, love—while her half-human, half-divine qualities (as goddess of the moon she was affiliated with the heavens, as goddess of wildlife she was identified with nature) refer her in Papatsonis's poem to Dante's Beatrice. Artemis possessed both healing and destructive powers like those of the Christian God, and was associated with the sun, being the sister of Apollo, who was known as Helios, or the Sun. In this aspect she was called Phoebe, the feminine form of Phoebus, the Sun. Like the Christian and Hebrew God, she had many names and was not considered an exclusively Hellenic goddess,[11] as Papatsonis recognized in his use of the figure in his poem.

Artemis's tripartite nature is clearly revealed in *Ursa Minor*. In the fourth poem of the work, "The Proclaimed," she is Hecate, "the livid form of death" which pales at the presence of the divine guide:

> she greatly lulls the turbulent
> and alleviates the irascible
> so that the livid
> form of death
> paled was consumed
> and at last completely abolished
> the Moon always fading
> until it vanished
> (81–88)

Death as a physical quality is here compared to the moon, which is diminished and eventually abolished in Kallisto's presence. The moon is pale, as is death; as it progresses from full to new moon, disappearing from the sight of man, so is death extinguished in the presence of the divine. In "Before a Journey" Artemis is again referred to as the moon:

> the roving one also lent relief
> which this evening was revealed more inclined
> to alchemy more bountiful
> and industrious
> (4–7)

This "roving one" is she whose fullness shed light on the firmament and who thus helped the poet find the hope he was seeking in the heavens. Artemis as the moon in "Before a Journey" is no longer a force of the underworld but a divine force functioning as the poet's guide, while in "The Attractions," the eighth part of *Ursa Minor*, she takes on her earthly aspect as the virgin huntress who feels the "whips of jealousy" at the approach of a rival in beauty:

> even the most arrogant Artemis
> first discerned the whips

of jealousy hearing enthroned
in her region Kallisto
so marvelous and full of flowers
(32–36)

VIII   *Kallisto and Aphrodite*

Through Artemis, Kallisto has been confused in Greek mythology with Aphrodite, the goddess of love. As Robert Graves
remarks, "the Olympian Artemis was more than a maiden. Elsewhere, at Ephesus, for instance, she was worshipped in her second
person as a Nymph, an orgiastic Aphrodite with a male con-
sort. . . ." [12] Papatsonis's desire to confuse Kallisto and Aphrodite
in his *Ursa Minor* is made clear in his "Chronicle of Endurance
and Suffering." He explains that in addition to selecting the myth
of Kallisto because of its association with Arcadia, he chose it
because of "the opposition and rivalries of Artemis, so as to result
in my personalized wartime divinity to confuse her with the same
solitary and proud Aphrodite." [13] The combination of Artemis and
Aphrodite in one figure identical with Kallisto is most evident in
the final poem of *Ursa Minor*, "The Attractions," in the passage
where evening approaches:

for the first time the hidden one appears to us
who until yesterday was still in the arms of day
detailing for us
—the roses belong to her—
this panarchaic queen of love
the enactment of her hegemony
(97–102)

The "hidden one" who first appears at the end of the day is the
moon which appeared earlier as "the roving one" ("Before a
Journey," 4). The moon is also she who assigns to us the roses,
flowers sacred to Aphrodite and the emblem of love. The figure
had earlier been described in the dancelike encircling of love in
lines 38–45:

your yoked beams
invite us irrevocably
to your seductive net crafted

> with golden threads
> your Dancers arabesque around you
> while you modestly
> nurture all the suns
> perpetuate their flames

Here the eyes of the goddess beckon us toward her nets, those in which her husband Hephesteus trapped the goddess and her lover Aries, the god of war. Her great beauty calls us to her, while around her dance the Seasons, daughters of Themis who circled about Aphrodite to adorn her as she arose naked from the sea. The suns about her increase in intensity ("perpetuate their flames"), being nurtured by her presence. The figure is later referred to as "this panarchaic queen of love," an identification followed in the poem by a quote from the third Homeric hymn to Aphrodite:

> she who presents humans
> with such nice presents
> that seductive face of hers
> is always smiling always
> carrying its seductive flower
> (103–107) [14]

Further described as one who, unafraid, twisted

> about the wild Lion's mane
> and gave to the Virgin's spika
> opposite its summer ripeness
> (116–118)

she is identified with the sun in its passage through the fifth sign of the zodiac, Leo the lion, and the sixth sign, Virgo, whose star pica is now in its summer fullness. Addressed as "directress of the stars / helmsman of the sun which binds us" (129–130, a reference to the polar star—the first star to appear in the heavens and thus a guide to all the others—which serves as the tip of Kallisto's constellation), Aphrodite, like Artemis, is tied through her relation to the sun with the nymph Kallisto, the poet's guide. It is Aphrodite's penultimate attribute as goddess of love which is used to culminate the whole *Ursa Minor* in its identification of God, love, sun, and the nymph-guide:

"from today love reigns" we tell you
"love reigns from today"
we shout it like marathon racers
having arrived hurriedly at life's threshold
but you doubt us
as an unfaithful implacable creation
and unaccustomed to revelations
we will thrust off your disbelief
because our announcements are true
etched with indisputable fire
be assured at last as we bring you the toil
of a squandered life
awaiting your acceptance of the knowledge
which this "reigns" conveys.

                    ("The Attractions," 132–145)

IX *Kallisto and the Fates*

Papatsonis reinforced the myth of Kallisto by using not only
elements of the myths of Artemis and Aphrodite, but also of the
myth of the Fates who have been associated in classical lore with
both Artemis and Aphrodite. The Fates had traditionally been
called *kalais kyrades*, "good ladies," recalling the name used for
Artemis in Aetolia, *e kyra kalo*, "the good lady" or "the lady beautiful," as well as the ancient name of Artemis, *kalliste*, "most
beautiful," from which epithet, it has been suggested, *Kallisto*
herself derived her name.[15] Papatsonis himself refers to the Fates
as *kales Moires*, "good fates" ("The Fates Lead," 95). Lawson
states that, "according to a fragment of Epimenides, 'golden Aphrodite and the deathless Fates' were daughters of Cyonos and
Euonyme. Their sisterly relation was recognized also in a cult.
Near the Ilius once stood a temple containing an old wooden
statue (*xoanon*) of heavenly Aphrodite with an inscription nam-
ing her 'eldest of the Fates' (*presvetera ton Moiron*)."[16] Robert
Graves suggests further that Aphrodite Urania was called "the
eldest of the Fates" because it was she to whom the king in ancient
times had been ritually sacrificed at the summer solstice. As
Graves notes, the Fates, like Artemis, were moon-goddesses whose
dresses were white robes and who spun linen thread: "Clotho is
the 'spinner,' Lachesis the 'measurer,' Atropos is 'she who cannot
be turned, or avoided.' Moera means 'a share' or 'a phase,' and
the moon has three phases and three persons; the new moon, the

maiden-goddess of the spring, the first period of the year; the full moon, the Nymph-goddess of the summer, the second period; and the old moon, the Crone-goddess of autumn, the last period." [17]

In "The Fates Lead," the sixth poem of *Ursa Minor*, the poet pictures the Fates as an "imposing army dressed in white" (115–116). In the same poem the Fates are introduced in connection with the moon which is presented in terms descriptive of Artemis—"scornful," "arrogant," "foreign":

> this evening as
> the broad idle moon
> loitered late upon us
> arrogant as always and if at times
> not entirely foreign only
> her scorn and indifference
> divides among us suddenly
> all the good fates appeared
> (88–95)

In this poem the universe beckons us constantly both during the night and the day; but we ignore her because we are not willing to leave our place on earth, our restricted region, to go beyond the physical self. The divine aid of the three Fates is provided to help the poet free himself from his physical bonds and enable him to open his soul to God:

> until heavenly women
> determined
> to arrange more expediently
> what our irresolute apathy beguiled
> (83–86)

The divine role of these heavenly women is later depicted in more specific terms:

> it won for us at last
> our hesitant resistance
> the confrontation of the great
> processional march as organized
> by the bewitching clouds
> in the plain of white hope
> and at the enticements
> of the tempestuous cape
> (119–126)

The coming of the Fates ("the great processional march") is organized by the heavens where hope reigns. We are no longer hesitant to leave our material world for the spiritual one of the soul. The revelation of the three divine guides has lifted us from our stupor, awakened us from our lethargy; bringing us face to face with God, it has enabled us to unite with Him. A confrontation is thus brought about by the heavens through the divine aid of the Fates and through the insistence of our internal agitation and frustration at knowing of a world beyond our present one which we are unable to reach. With the Fates to show us the path to the spiritual world, Fates who come from God, man has nothing to fear:

> now that the fates lead
> and such fates
> like ours
> all-powerful fates
> with them necessity immediately declines
> complaint with them unravels
> bitterness loses power
> (130–136)

X   Conclusion

The relatively simple feminine presence of Papatsonis's shorter poems is complicated in *Ursa Minor* through the consolidation of many female guides in the figure of Kallisto. Like her earlier counterparts, Kallisto is a virgin—half-human, half-divine—one desired by the poet and yet inaccessible to him. She arrives in moments of darkness, bringing a joyous light with her to guide man to his Creator. She calms man, protects him from sin, brings him hope and faith, and promises him love. She is a magnet that enlightens, "burns, with the touch of Love." Unseen but felt, her presence is understood through man's sensuous contacts with nature, for Kallisto takes on the form of the natural elements, as well as the form of various other guiding figures, to clothe her abstract and ineffable essence.

But Kallisto is a much larger figure than those who appeared in earlier poems. She is an intervening force in its highest and most detailed expression. Representing the resolution of all contradictions, she is many things in one: the martyred innocent, the Queen, the Mother, the Loved One. She is patient suffering, endurance, and faith rewarded. As her symbolic function has been intensified, she is now presented in analogies to Christ, God, Mary, classical Virgin goddesses, and the sun, taking on at once a triple and a double nature: the three aspects of the trinity and of Artemis (as Luna the moon goddess, Diana the nature goddess, and Hecate, goddess of Hell); the double nature—human and divine—of Christ, the Virgin Mary, and Dante's Beatrice.

In Kallisto the whole drama of man's journey from sin to salvation is played out; she trumpets the resurrection as a fixed star in the heavens, guiding man in his escape from the hell of years of war and the inadequacy of his temporal existence along the inalterable road of struggle and denial that leads to the splendidly brilliant light of the source of love. It is in this multiform female presence, Kallisto, that Papatsonis has achieved the most complex expression of the female figure who passes through all periods of his poetry.

CHAPTER 4

Style and Imagery

PAPATSONIS'S most mature poetry is characterized stylistically by its failure to use a strict verse form, its discontinous and dreamlike combination of images, and its highly personal quality. It is a poetry which intends to elicit meaning rather than to lend itself to pyrotechnical effects, a poetry limited in specific poetic patterns and devices. Papatsonis's verse does not incorporate obvious metrical schemes, though, as the poet states, it utilizes patterns of rhythms and sounds to make the meaning more emphatic.[1]

Papatsonis's language is that of the mystical poet whose obscurity is to a large extent conditioned by his transformation of myth and symbol into philosophy in surreallike images which express the flow of the subconscious. A religious poet, he is, nevertheless, neither canonical nor schematic; rather, his poetry is deeply spiritual, infused with visionary language and images. Though there is an apparent dichotomy between the surreallike and the religious or theological aspects of his poetry, the poet resolves it in the highly mystical lyric outpouring of feeling that occurs in his best poetry.

One of the greatest difficulties posed by the poet's works lies in his special use of the Greek language. Studied in the nuances of a language which has a continuous history of some thousands of years, Papatsonis writes in qualified high demotic, or spoken Greek, a form of the language which in his poetry is periodically attended by Katharevousa, the artificial literary language of modern Greece, as well as by some classical and Byzantine Greek. The latter is used, as the poet has himself indicated, "for atmosphere," [2] though clearly its use is intended to demonstrate Papatsonis's own conviction that the literary and social heritage of contemporary Christian Greece originates most completely in the Byzantine era.

[90]

Papatsonis's work is tempered further by a conscious person-alization of his poetry to comment on problems of his own times, a tendency exhibited most successfully in his poems "V Day," "The Lamentation of a Greek for the Martyrdom and the Con-demnation of Joseph Mindzenty," and "I Sing the Wrath." Papat-sonis contends, in this regard, that poetry must maintain a "living contact and organic relation with the society that brought it forth." [3] It is partially for this reason that his highly individual images are often, like Ezra Pound's, both difficult to decipher and lacking in clarity.

Perhaps the most determined characteristics of Papatsonis's poetry, qualities enhanced by the poet's general disinterest in for-mal rhythmic and metrical schemes, are, as Kimon Friar indicates, "the language and rhythm of deduction and prose statement."[4] The poet's own aesthetic dictates that substance determine poetry, that matter must, in the end, predominate over form. It is in de-fense of this concept that Papatsonis, in a personal interview, cited Plato and Nietzsche as great poets, for clearly their work abounds in substantive matter. The transformation of myth into philosophy in their work is itself a poetic virtue, for, Papatsonis claims, beauty lies not in the techniques of poetry but in the vision that infuses it. "What do I care," he wrote in *Ellenika Phylla* (1935), "if the image is anarchic, ugly, uncultivated. The faith and vision dominate me, because these are the qualities that make the poet." [5]

It is this very determination of Papatsonis to rely heavily in his poetry on vision and philosophy that leads him to seek in his longest and finest work, *Ursa Minor*, a symmetry which would structure the work formally, leaving him free to explore through his language, imagery, and rhythms those philosophical concerns which preoccupy him. His "lady" in *Ursa Minor* appears at the structural center of that work. The poems cluster into groups of one, three, one, three. The first poem stands alone as an intro-duction to the whole, the next three as analogous to the *Inferno*, the fifth poem as a *Purgatorio*, and the last three as a *Paradiso*. Each poem is further divided into three thematically different parts, though not necessarily of equal length.

Other of his poems, being shorter and restricted to the develop-ment of a single theme, exhibit little structural symmetry apart from the balanced rhythm of the lines. It is largely in the poems of 1910–1919 that simple patterns are used; the "Military Songs," for example, are written in four-line rhymed verses. In the bulk of his poetry structural devices appear only periodically. In some cases, such as in the poem "Her Agitation and Serenity," 1953, the poem is divided into two parts, here titled "I. Responsibility" and "II. Innocence"; while a poem such as "The Worship of the Idol," 1945, is simply divided into twelve parts of from seven to twenty-one lines each.

I *Imagery*

Papatsonis's best poems, however, are given form by a single image which dominates the poem and which often breaks off into related image clusters. A simple, almost prosaic use of a dominent image appears in "The Thread," 1949, in which the poet's path is guided to where all roads converge. Unaware of the nature of his journey, but guided like the Magi by the stars, he finds his way to the Nativity, knowing only that

> to all, whether alert or whether
> they lay surrendered to their indolence,
> the Presence outside was persistently wandering,
> the unsleeping essence of a life-giving night
> in which something was being conceived or had been born:
> something not written down, something missing
> from the huge pages of the Census Taker—something—
>   a thread,
> which delicately bound all things together into one body
>   (46–53) °

The thread (Christ), like the path and the stars, gathers together the varied strains of life into a single body. The poet, uncertain of all, weaves his way like a thread himself to this "least portion of earth" (2)° having something special to impart which "had not/properly matured within me yet, nor even formed" (25–26).° The Presence wanders too, both it and the poet bearing meaning that binds all paths into one.

More complicated dominant images occur in the woman of the carnations in "A Fearless Woman Dressed in Many Carnations," the hunt for the soul in "The Quarry," the thread of the Fates in "The Fates Lead," the birds in "Before a Journey," the hours in "The Petrified Insect," the great magnet of the sun in "The Attractions," and the stellar system in "The Proclaimed" and "Faith and Hope." The dominant image in these poems is usually not permitted to dominate until the conclusion of the poem. The image is merely suggested initially, and, as the poem proceeds, fragmentary and seemingly unrelated images are introduced, distracting the reader from the primary image and creating an effect of puzzlelike pieces which cannot be understood in terms of an organic unit until the threads are knit together in the final dominance of the major image.

The poems thus take on a radiating quality, for from their initiating impulse they burst open like the rose of Dante's *Paradiso* (a dominant image in *Ursa Minor*, especially in the dedication) into a pattern of diverging rays of images. Though the rays are tied to the essential core of meaning, they are not revealed to be interrelated through the central motif or image until late in the poem when the poem has exhausted its potential and resolved its varied streams. In "A Fearless Woman Dressed in Many Carnations," the major image of carnations is identified with a springlike happiness and then referred to in an image of pain and blood which is gradually specified as the wounds of war. The beautiful woman is introduced as wearing the flowers, only to be displaced by images of the blooming of the flower in the barrel of a rifle and the flaring up of the flower in the mouth. The woman is subsequently depicted as bleeding for man, an image supplanted by one of a garden of shed petals and dried-up cherry trees, and is finally referred to in the closing stanza as a red icon of carnations, a "beloved Erinys / the bloodstained" (126–127).

It is only in the final stanza that all the pieces of the puzzle are united. The woman is transformed from one beloved for her beauty to one admired for her fury and the taking on of man's bloody wounds. In this last verse the images of red carnations, blood, Kallisto, the Savior, and the Erinys come together into a single unit of meaning which, in retrospect, informs the poem as a whole, joining its fragmentary parts into a coherent entity.

Papatsonis's diversions from the line of thought which is pursued in a poem often seem to explore what seems an unrelated image, though it is one which forms, in fact, a progression relevant to the mosaic pattern of the whole. A good example of such an image in its most mature form occurs in "Faith and Hope":

a sprig of flowered thyme
was formerly a monumental expectation
and now it becomes
largely an object of the sea
which blesses us with the shoreline's dew
and its colorless tone exhumed it
from sandy shores
(23–29)

In the midst of a discussion of the evening as a revealer of God's presence, the poet turns to this image of the thyme, an image which functions in its own right as a poem within the poem. But the dampened pale thyme as an instrument of blessing and a symbol of the resurrection expresses the awakening of the divinity of man in the darkness of the night. The image thus permits both an extension of the poem's meaning and an opportunity to explore new dimensions and to embroider new patterns.

II *Visual Images*

Papatsonis's individual images are in many instances visual. Separated from the whole, they can often stand as individual units, like small icons or paintings, a quality which Papatsonis admired in Dante's work as he indicates in an essay in which he compares some of Dante's passages to works of the painter Giotto.[6] The image of the hunt in "The Quarry" provides an example in Papatsonis's work of visual images:

nor did these holidays occur
without decorations and ornamentations
next to the principal heroes
our dancing hunting dogs
commendable breeds beautiful lines
magical movements and the horses
much more admirable and majestic
and the environ
whether forested mountainous or aquatic
varying each time in its manner
the appropriate seasons shifting
recurring in their own delight
that we might reside in the lingering
fantasticism of an elevated actuality
(21–34)

The hunt, the poet explains, will not attract spectators or hunters unless decorations and ornaments attend the affair. The poet pauses to note the beauty of the hunting dogs—all hand-picked for such a holiday—and the horses, more impressive than even the dogs. The party of hunters is accoutered in costumes which are changed, depending upon the place of the hunt and upon the different seasons which themselves impose variations on the hunt. The hunt creates the impression of an "elevated actuality," another world in which one occasionally catches a fleeting vision of the stag as it disappears in confusion within the shadows of the forest.

Through the imagery of the hunt, the poet is concerned with man's quest for God, or the soul, which is represented by Kallisto. In this poem the quest takes on the qualities of a hunt where the quarry, the stag, is the soul or the beloved that man is trying to reach. The poet demonstrates in the hunt man's emphasis on the material in his quest for the spiritual. Man, says Papatsonis, must seek God through faith, grappling with his unconscious in order to find Him rather than treating God as external to himself in order to avoid inner struggle. Man, however, becomes so interested in the pomp and glory of external ceremonies that ritual itself becomes more important than the actual object of the hunt, and it takes on an aspect of higher reality itself. Man feels he rises to God, though the ritual itself is not the way to God but merely a means of glimpsing Him only for a moment, after which He disappears, dissolving with the end of the ritual.

"Attic Shapes," 1940, provides an example of one type of the poet's visual poems. As Kimon Friar indicates by appending to his translation of the poem an inscription from Keats's "Ode on a Grecian Urn," it is a work close in spirit to its English predecessor:

> Now the balance is shaken; now one of the scales
> dips down towards the abyss, the other kicks high,
> for the disk which holds the Night grows heavy
> while the Day is as weightless as a bird.
> If the inclination swerve much further down,
> we shall see the balance standing straight
> instead of finding its equilibrium, as we had expected,
> pointing with its lever in a vertical line:
> as when resistance has waned

and the counterweight vanishes in an assumption
—such an immaterial ascension, and so luminous!
. . . .
Where every day the inexhaustible light
is drawn and scattered in an Attic corner,
exquisite Hymettos at its ridges overbrims
with feathery clouds that linger on its slopes.
That is not the menacing Hood of the storm rising,
where the daintily-haired Demigoddess of the Sea reclines
and combs her hair, but the bucolic playfulness of the Sun.
A slow, surpassing flute, slowly and barely audible
in the surrounding regions, restrains all astonished
        creatures
to an absolute serenity—the near affinity of Harmony.

Fleeting and God-sent Blissful Weather stands by her
        side.
No matter how brief, this is a moment of eternity,
utter abolition of the tumescent Night,
triumphal Songs of Victory, bud ready to flower
beyond the Law, gift of God, negation of Winter.
                        (1–11; 30–44) °

Like Keats's poem, Papatsonis's work is preoccupied with the
frozen motion of shapes whose moment of eternity has been
ensured. His focus in these passages ranges from the equilibrious
balance of Day and Night to the overbrimming ridges of "exquisite Hymettos" and the "feathery clouds that linger on its
slopes." He speaks elsewhere in the poem of personalized nature,
of the hands of day which lift to touch the moon, the azure
awakening and the wondrous nakedness of the nymphs of the
sea. A breeze of light brings ripples to a spring morning, while
"indolent Day" proffers the spring its transcendency.

Papatsonis's physical response in "Attic Shapes" to what he calls
in the poem "immaterial" ideas is expressed in the material envel-
opment of the abstract in his poetry in general. The visual or
painterly quality in Papatsonis's images is created to a large extent by the poet's concretization of the abstract, a recurring device
throughout his poetry and one which characterizes the poet's attempt to make tangible the intangible. Individual images are built
on sensual details: in *Ursa Minor* the "crooked nails of barren
love" ("The Petrified Insect," 102–103), the "musk tree of our

hell" (The Petrified Insect," 98), the quarry "with its many-braided horns / and its tight dully lit eyes" ("The Quarry," 37–38), the "scented cloud which extends / its dissatisfied wandering breath" ("A Fearless Woman Dressed in Many Carnations," 40–41). Larger clusters of sensual images function in the poems as central configurations: the procession of the three Fates, that of the chariot of the sun and the ceremony of the hunt, for example.

The treatment of images as word-pictures to convey states of mind in terms of concrete and static visual images is exemplified in "The Fates Lead," lines 63–69. The image of night as developed in this passage also provides an example of the mosaiclike structure of Papatsonis's poetry:

> the Chinese ink
> night's indelible darkness
> that we might write the thousand and one nights
> of our future history
> and decorate the phantom
> teachings of Chuang-Tzu
> life's talismans

The night in its darkness and apparent permanence is likened to Chinese ink, a material necessary if man is to write of his struggle toward the soul. The reference to writing, and specifically to Chinese ink, is continued in the introduction of the Taoist philosopher Chuang-Tzu, thus tying the darkness of the night, the written history of man's struggle, and the lessons of the Taoist into a unit. The relation of these elements, however, is that of discontinuous images given meaning by a careful laying out of seemingly unrelated parts until the pieced-together puzzle suggests a coherent world of its own.

A less complicated, though more complete, joining of images showing Papatsonis's concretization of the abstract appears in "The Petrified Insect":

> once in the all-round
> nights
> and the hours when
> earth's silence is undone
> when the new birds
> are summoned

> to deliver oracles
> then as the birds'
> bills aggravate
> the bleeding
> open wounds
> of our doubts
> then as the birds'
> bills entangle
> the yarn of our schemes
> (45–59)

Here the nights are all-round ones, like a ball of yarn, complete, dark, ideal for the meditation of the soul. The silence of the night is "undone" to provide for meditation, just as ideas, beliefs, are disentangled by understanding. The birds which appear are new thoughts summoned during the silence of the night to deliver new understanding, to probe our doubts (the open wounds) and make them bleed. The two images—that of the yarn and that of the birds—are joined in the last lines of the passage where the birds probing our open wounds entangle with their bills the ball of yarn, our enmeshed ideas, our questioning being.

In both the above images, a tableau is created much like that of a surrealist painting in which varied concrete objects are used to treat abstract states of mind. The creation of picturelike images recurs throughout *Ursa Minor* in much the same manner. At times the abstract is made concrete in such a way that other image-pictures are suggested, as in "The Petrified Insect":

> at times this southwesterly wind
> that scavenges us appears
> erupting its fury upon us
> the etesian wind's caress
> (5–8)

In this passage the personified wind sweeps upon us as someone about to do us harm. In the context of the whole poem the south wind is identified with Kallisto, the guide who sweeps upon us in a violent caress. But the image refers as well to the myth of Kallisto in which Zeus came upon the nymph in just such a forceful manner. The image is an ecstatic one in which the south wind, Kallisto, as part of a greater wind, God (the annual northerly etesian wind) sweeps upon us in love, "erupting its fury upon us," just as Zeus overcame the nymph Kallisto in his obsession with her beauty.

In the same poem the hours are made concrete through association with a ceremony of blessing in the Greek Orthodox service:

> they are thus attuned
> the miraculous hours
> blessed with a moistened
> basil spray
> (14–17)

The hours represent the faithful who are "blessed with a moistened/basil spray" during Holy Week. Thus the hours are blessed ones, for they have been anointed by the holy water of the basil. They are "miraculous hours," they are never-ending, decreasing and increasing, exhausting themselves and being reconstituted as they diminish and expand, "aerified by their pulse's spinning top" (11). As the top spins, the seconds, represented by its turns, are aerified, emerging as part of the atmosphere that makes up all the other seconds which have met the same fate. This cycle is a never-ending one in which time exhales itself into the great source of life, increasing and becoming whole again by inhaling its being from it. At times these hours are seen as living plants:

> and all bloom
> they flourish
> and form
> the Olympian perfection
> (19–22)

Elsewhere the morning hours are personified as women who, hanging out their linen in the morning,

> hurl their rays
> and their morning linen
> to cloak all things
> (36–38)

In an image of night, Papatsonis again uses personification in a rather visual way: "the serene nights fall unfolding/gold wealth on black fabric" ("The Proclaimed," 50–51). Here night approaches as something human, something concrete and animated which unfolds itself as an old woman might the bundle she carries to reveal all her belongings. The night unfolds its bundle to reveal the "gold wealth" of the stars, the light of the stars that is seen only after night has spread across the heavens.

At times these picture-images take on a rich dreamlike quality, as in lines 100–118 from "The Fates Lead":

> immediately the wild pigeons burst forth
> playing and revelling crazily
> vaulting drunkenly
> so much that the night from being
> mellifluous became at once
> a windy threshing-floor plucking
> in the encounter their down in abundance
> and forcing it
> into a course aroused
> by all the flock and clews
> which the fates in their wakefulness
> bestrewed carding
> their sheep's fleece
>
> how had our sleep begun
> what mist consumed it
> what imposing army
> dressed in white
> what deep hidden goodness
> annihilated it with fiery amazement

The poet views man contemplating his soul in the recesses of the night under the influence of God's nightly messengers. He treats the vision as a mystical one which finds its roots in classical mythology, Christian symbols, and Greek folklore. Thus, on a Greek village threshing-floor a flock of pigeons (the pigeon is an image of the soul in Orthodox iconography) flies frantically about, being plucked by the fury of the wind. On the periphery of the circle sit three old women carding the wool of their sheep. They are the Fates preparing the string that measures out the life of man. As the pigeon feathers rise, they are united with the discarded flakes and continue up to the heavens. The sheep from which the string originates are a symbol of Christ, indicating both the divine source of man's fate and union with God during the night of the soul.

As this discussion indicates, Papatsonis does not always detail his visual images, nor are they specifically related to a clear narrative purpose. Rather, his visual images are sometimes terse and dreamlike in nature. Often arbitrarily juxtaposed to contrasting images to create a disjointed effect, these images are pleasurable in their exoticism rather than in any defined and constricted function. Recognizing the need to make his often abstract world comprehensible on a concrete level to his readers, Papatsonis tries to make his images visual and specific, without compromising their surreallike quality or their intensely mystical purpose. An example of just such a stylistic combination occurs as early as 1921 in "Daniel in Fovea Leonum Signata":

> Brown manes, monstrous thunderbolts, majestic flashes,
> fear and terror in the darkness and on certain deathly
>   nights,
> nails of steel, hatchways of striking mouths,
> pits within pits, as many dark moments as might await
>   me,
> worse than the seven-times more powerful furnace of my
>   three brothers.
> And in this way we will enter triumphantly your holy
>   Temple. And whatever is going to be let it be.
>
> On the highest tower of my home, three nights vigilant,
>   three days
> a faster, in the clouds, in the stars, in the tempests,
>   in the skies
> I could see a vision of Upper Jerusalem enormously
>   spread out
> with God's Christ tearful, with my luckless King Joachim
> and with the wise Darius, the victor, propagating dogmas
> concerning the Persians, concerning his idols. The Lions
> meanwhile roared imprisoned in their den.
>   (1–13)

The disembodied manes, nails, and mouths awaiting Daniel in the darkness of the den are contrasted to his vision in the tower of a tearful Christ arising out of the tempests of Upper Jerusalem. The imminence of Daniel's trial is foreseen in the "monstrous thunderbolts, magnetic flashes" of the "deathly nights," though it is not specified by the poet. The impending battle is treated rather as a nightmarish dream which combines both the concrete features of the real event and the supernatural aspects of his mystical vision.

"Christmas of Tears," 1930, presents a more metaphysical version of Papatsonis's surreallike visions, joining together pagan and Christian elements and moving from the worldly to the unworldly with fluency:

> Vainly you ask for a well of happiness,
> a small oasis in a boundless Hades
> in which you revolve, a sandy Hades,
> in which with every step the foot
> sinks further than the knee
> creating fatigue for the engaged
> Future which awaits you
> when the body can no longer endure.
> The hallucination of a small rain
> two or three drops, a blessing
> it would have been, for you a new Baptism,
> a thousand hopes it would relate to you.
> But the one Sun's endless revolutions
> wither happiness.
> . . . .
> For me it was set up on the spur of the moment
> as "The Place of the Skull." A circle
> of crosses have encircled me, I should select
> the lightest and depart,
> to be hung by the iniquitous
> Jewesses, these monstrous Conceptions.
>
> The Sibyl took fire,
> and foretold what is written for me.
>   (15–28; 37–44)

The Sibyl in this poem prophesies the poet's destiny, bridging for him the gap between the pagan and the Christian worlds— between that of "a small oasis in a boundless Hades" and "the garden of consolation" (54). The images developed range from man's being swallowed up by the earth as he revolves in his "sandy" land to his being encircled by crosses in "The Place of the Skull" waiting to be hung by "iniquitous Jewesses." The poet again presents us with a strange landscape of monstrous events which are themselves physically palpable, but which carry us into a world beyond the natural, one which is all the more frightening for its roots in material reality.

III   *Childlike Joy*

In conjunction with the sometimes simple visual nature of his poetry, Papatsonis's images often depict a childlike exhuberance and joy, a quality the poet much admired in the *Commedia* as he indicates in his essay "A Triptych from Dante's *Paradiso*." Commenting on Canto XXIV, Papatsonis contends that the innocence, simplicity, sense of accomplishment, and the naive youthful pleasure expressed by Dante are paralleled by those which occur in Byzantine icons—especially in the icons of the birth and crucifixion of Christ—in which small childlike details are included, details which were later, unfortunately, to embarrass the monks of Mount Athos who made the icons.[7] It is a similar kind of joy that is found in Papatsonis's poetry. It occurs when Papatsonis speaks of nature through the eyes of innocence, capitalizing simple words just as a child might in order to emphasize something of importance to himself. In "Before the Advent" (1918), the poet describes in this manner the unhampered freedom of the animals he finds wandering about him:

> And the dumb beasts, the Hens and the Hares,
> the Pigeons and the Bats, wander freely in the Bushes;
> the Honeybees sing, and the Snails,
> after the rain, proceed in their Easter Barouches.
>   (9–12) *

In this poem, the poet stands outside a garden "lush with fountains and flowers" (3) waiting for the "Great Gate" (4) to open and admit him. The gate is that to the Garden of Eden which the poet hopes to enter, but which he knows will be closed to him because of his past sins. As he walks, he watches the small animals running about without care and realizes that only he is alone. The poet's admiration of these animals is treated with the joy and vitality of a child whose eyes have grown big at watching the work of nature.

This youthful quality is again evident in "The Ships and Other Things," 1929, where the poet deals with God's whole creation. He describes the sun of the day and the moon and the stars of

the night. He finds pleasure in the trees, buds, and insects. Like
a child, he begins to seek in plants a voice corresponding to that
of the animals:

> In every species of plant there is a corresponding
> voice.
> The voice of the Donkey, for instance, corresponds
> to Cypress Trees.
> The voice of the Owl, to Olive Trees. Of the Cock
> to Olive Trees again.
> Of the Turkey Hen, of the Wasp, to Thorns or to Grapes.
> (9–12) **

Here again the names of the animals are capitalized in a primitive
childlike picture, a quality of Papatsonis's poetry which Kimon
Friar comments on in the introduction to his *Modern Greek
Poetry*: "Nature is seen through the eyes of a child pure and fresh,
and yet as strangely evocative as a canvas by Rousseau or the
Greek primitive painter Theophilos; such is the description, in
capital letters, of the flora and fauna of the Garden of Eden in
'Before the Advent'." [8]

A "pure and fresh vision," [9] as the Greek critic Cleon Paraschos
describes this quality in Papatsonis's poetry, remains with the
poet throughout his career. It is evident in the *Ursa Minor*, although by the time of its composition the poet does not capitalize
as freely as previously; his vitality begins to express itself in other
ways. "Before a Journey," for example, pictures the poet's joy in
nature in a more restrained manner:

> a skylark
> takes the lead
> assumes their leadership
> more forcibly and impetuously
> a warbler awakening
> is jealous
> meanwhile it secretly gnaws itself
> seeing wasted
> its dawn's laudations
> the geraniums become wild
> how can they endure
> our love's retreat
> so far away
> (88–100)

The passage introduces the skylark which is to take over leadership of a flight to God; rising higher as it sings, it suggests the
lead taken by loftier thoughts as they rise toward the heavens
singing praises to God. The lightheartedness of the passage is
expressed in the sense of life and animation with which the different parts of nature are endowed. The skylark playfully takes
over the leadership from other competing birds as the warbler
becomes jealous that Nature's attention is focused elsewhere.
The geraniums respond in a wild way at all the movement and
gaiety expressed around them.

Such playfulness can be seen throughout *Ursa Minor*. At times
it appears as the "dolphins' dance" and the fishes' leap following
the "naked joy" of the prow of a ship ("The Proclaimed," 127–
129). It can be seen in the pleasure of wild pigeons just released
from their cages "playing and dancing crazily/jumping drunk-
enly" ("The Fates Lead," 101–102), and in the grace of a rose:

> each of its petals a virtue
> every thorn a sting
> each thorn a grace
> one hundred
> the botanists call its joys
> and we thousands
> ("The Fates Lead," 25–30)

The whole universe becomes for Papatsonis a playground where
he, the child, is allowed to wander in unrestrained freedom and
to enjoy all that is contained. His universe is one filled with
revelry:

> the great universe for us
> and joy the universe
> and its revels
> ("The Fates Lead," 19–21)

All of creation bubbles in innocent enthusiasm as the poet par-
takes of the pleasures of the universe which "throb and vibrate"
("The Petrified Insect," 3).

Kallisto the beloved is herself presented in a playful, childlike
way. In "Faith and Hope" she is the "gymnast of our dreams"
(38). In "The Quarry" she is seen as "bounding multicolored/

happy and cunning." She is the tiger, leopard, or lioness (82–88) whom the poet desires to wrestle so that he may be strengthened in the fight. Elsewhere she "shouts and laughs / dances and resounds" in guiltless jubilation ("The Proclaimed," 37–38) as she appears in the evening as the constellation Ursa Minor. When the poet is overjoyed by the love he feels engulfing him, as in "The Attractions," he creates a rhyming riddle to express the swelling of love within him:

> in summer shaped
> in August grows
> by St. Demetrius' pledged
> by Christmas glows
> (84–88)

It is this overbrimming exuberance which Papatsonis feels toward Nature and the universe that enables him to defeat his doubts and to journey toward the heavens. Like Dante, bursting with child-like happiness, the poet rises ever higher toward the Empyrean.

IV *Twist Ending*

Among the poetic devices periodically used by Papatsonis is the twist ending, a device commonly found in Cavafy's poetry, to which Papatsonis devoted some study. As used by Cavafy, the twist ending involves a radical altering of the direction of the poem in its last lines to state a proposition whose inevitability and whose rightness strikes the reader with a shock of recognition that sets the poem in a new and more significant dimension. This effect is achieved largely through an encapsulating image or set of images clarifying the true subject of the poem, in some cases changing the direction of the poem and placing it in a new and more startling perspective, and in others merely providing the poem with a more intense expression of its meaning.

In Papatsonis's early poems one finds similarly achieved effects, particularly in "Annetoula," 1913; "To a Young Girl Brought Up in a Nunnery," 1919; and "Summer Tourists Go to Mass in Piraeus," 1929. In "Annetoula," one of his earliest poems, the poet makes use of an extended simile in which he compares subject A to subject B:

> Like a Deacon solemnly attired
> who comes forth dressed in the Spirit
> of a Holy Angel, apotheosized
> drunkenly in the waves of incense
> raising the Holy Bread
> above his guiltless head
> (and from fear and respect his face
> is silver-coated with moonlike paleness)
> I too wish some tranquil morning
> then when the delights of Autumn begin
> to offer you my love in the midst of the
> bewildering uproar of a noted organ
> and in the shape of a holy,
> devotional and golden Gift, O beloved Girl.

The Deacon, subject B, is presented first, described largely by the solemnity of his faith for eight of the fourteen lines of the poem. Subject A, the poet himself, expresses his admiration of the mystery and pomp of such a service and desires to demonstrate his own love in the same manner. Until the last line, however, one does not know who this revered object is, though one assumes it must be God since all the images are religious. The last line gives the poem a new twist and clarifies its meaning as the poet utters, "O beloved Girl," exposing the poet's use of a religious metaphor to express his erotic love for a woman, Annetoula.

"To A Young Girl Brought Up in a Nunnery" presents a different form of ending from "Annetoula." It presents a young nun who, preoccupied with thoughts of God, permits the terror of the storm outside to enter and pass through her. The simple though bizarre situation is thrown into a new light by the last stanza, where the poet calls on Tranquility to adhere to the lesson taught by the nun and not to abandon the poet in the midst of a savage sea, but to engulf him. The meaning of the poem is intensified in these last lines, for the nun is elevated to a symbol of the calm of God at the heart of the storm of evil, one moved only by the "mild mutations of nature":

> O Tranquility, thou who art moved
> by the mild mutations of nature only,
> thou who dependendst on the existence of God Himself,
> abandon me not in the coming Winter

to be tossed about on the savage billows of the Sea:
throw me the end of a rope to haul me in.
(24–29) °

In "Summer Tourists Go to Mass in Piraeus," the poet again
concentrates on the intensification of his poem in the last lines:

On Ascension Day during morning Mass
a crowd of tourists rushed to the Cathedral,
from the ship *San Gervasi*. Burghers of Wurtemberg.
Summer tourists. It had been hot since morning.
They entered like a wave. They brought disorder.

Alone and unperturbed the Cathedral
held to its Hours. Proceeded with its Canons.
On the whole it governed like God Himself, and embraced
all of the faithful together, wherever they were.
Within the Inner Sanctum all
was Apostolic Law and Moderation.
The discords of the moment touched
the Indivisible Order not at all.°

Though the group of tourists rushing to Mass on Ascension Day
enters the cathedral like a wave of disorder, it cannot disrupt the
"Inner Sanctum." The reason is left suspended until the last lines
which explain, in a more abstract manner than has been adopted
throughout the poem, that the temporal in all its chaotic force
cannot affect the eternal.

In these three poems one finds Papatsonis using the ending of
a poem to alter its meaning in different ways. In "Annetoula" he
speaks of erotic love behind the veil of an image of divine love,
ironically revealing his intent only at the end. In "Summer Tourists Go to Mass in Piraeus," he deepens the meaning of a worldly
image by setting it in the end in a higher spiritual context. The
image in this poem becomes a higher version of itself as opposed
to the method of "Annetoula" where the first meaning of an image
is ironically reversed. Similarly in "To a Young Girl Brought Up
in a Nunnery," the poet shows the nun at the end of the poem
to be an abstract symbol rather than a real person, a deeper
spiritual version of the worldly or material image established
earlier by the poet.

As Papatsonis's work develops, as he become more obscure

and mystical, the greater complexity of his structure makes it more difficult to identify his use of this Cavafian device in his poems. The twist in Papatsonis's poetry becomes less pronounced, never as ironic as that found in Cavafy. His endings become more elaborately tied into the whole and work away from the directness more common to Cavafy. Nevertheless, it is characteristic of the subtleness of the poet's style that he grows to utilize this rather simple technique with greater and greater skill until in his most important composition, *Ursa Minor*, it becomes central to an understanding of the work.

In the seventh poem of *Ursa Minor*, "The Petrified Insect," Papatsonis exhibits his most mature use of this Cavafian mode. It is the last eighteen lines which serve both as a measure of the poem and as a higher, more concentrated rendering of it in a new set of figures which explain the poet's use of images throughout the poem, introducing at the same time a surprising new understanding of the meaning of the poem. The ending is thus a new and complete form in itself as well as the key to the unravelling of the perplexing whole which preceded it. In the final lines of the poem, the poet reveals that a tropical God has been exhumed, an ancient form culled up, resurrected from a hidden past:

> this is what we learned
> and will learn
> this is what the birds said
> the morning before we brought ourselves
> to the enigmatic worshippings
> of our tropical godliness
> which we exhumed from sphinxes
> the hard petrified insect
> does not reveal its secret
> as much as it is carved
> with scratches of worship
> the responsible magic stigma
> for all your transitions
> the image of the merciless cannonball
> which impregnates love
> the icon of creation
> as it pulsates
> in the passion of its ignition.
>   (209–226)

The exhumation of the secret has appeared as a motif in the poem in lines 124–126 as an idol worn erect at the tip of the hours, an iridescent, multigleaming, many-sided diamond excavated from the depths of man's aspirations—images in which the idea of godliness lies largely in the suggestions of the light-giving and many-faceted nature of the idol. In these last lines, however, the exhumed entity is "the hard petrified insect . . . carved with scratches of worship" which does not in the end tell its secret. The image of scratching, too, has appeared before in the poem, in line 190, but again in a different association. The fire of God is scratched behind the sound of the shriek of prayer, the monosyllabic exclamation of God's name. The image, reconstituted for use in the final section, shifts in meaning, though the sacred associations accumulate through repetition, throwing light on each other. Here, however, the nature of the scratched deity is revealed to us: it is the scarab, a symbol of the secrets of the soul and a talisman. The revelation both shocks and clarifies, for, though it substantiates the unexpected exhumation of the deity, it announces, ironically, the burial of the hope of its secret.

Finally, the last stanza of the poem represents a miniature world of its own, for it reflects the quest of *Ursa Minor* as a whole. Moving its focus, as does the whole poem, from man as questioning agent (209–215) to the soul as the refuser of life's secrets (216–219), and then to the nature of God Himself in His many manifestations (220–226), the last lines of the poem present God in the most critically significant forms He has taken in *Ursa Minor*; they express in culminating images the metaphors of Godliness as fire and force, God as passionately ignited and as a "merciless cannonball" (222). In this way the ending of "The Petrified Insect" represents Papatsonis's highest and most complex expression of the twist ending; it expresses both the placing of the poem in a new perspective (with the revelation of the scarab) and the intensification of its meaning (as a reconstitution in miniature of the journey encompassed by the whole eight-part work).

V   *Unifying Images*

Unique to Papatsonis's style is his ability to use his imagery as a unifying device in his longer poems, as exemplified in his handling of imagery throughout the whole of *Ursa Minor*. The concepts,

for example, of burial, exhumation, and resurrection are expressed
not only as primary images in the seventh poem, but as secondary
images in the second and third poems of *Ursa Minor*:

> how can I acknowledge now
> such a life replete
> which sufficed us then
> at the time of our mythical lethargy
>
> until you trumpeted
> your awakening triumph
> the end and our resurrection
> ("The Quarry," 49–55)

> and united at last we will form
> the earth's new summer day
> the longest of the year
> in the year of our love
> in the solstices of the year
> of the world's greatest love
> in those so inexperienced and unfamiliar
> portions of life
> which poor bewildered men were accustomed
> to call "mythical"
> and of which through suffering
> we were able to find the imprints
> and wounded we tracked them
> and arrived to find the marble
> idol of beauty
> soulless as it was and buried
> yet it stirred at our coming
> took life rekindled
> remained beautiful touched us
> and won us over.
> ("Faith and Hope," 89–108)

The buried one is expressed as the spark unsleeping in the depths
of our heart, as the most shining diamond in the deepest layers
of our aspirations, as our tropical godliness exhumed from
the grasp, as the soulless marble idol of beauty which took breath
in our coming. The exhumed is expressed as a petrified beauty
but also as "your awakening triumph / the end and our resurrection." Extending the image, the poet looks forward to the coming
of the gleaming presence, the "monumental expectation" ("Faith

and Hope," 2') of that which both resurrects and is itself resurrected:

> but at last you came
> the flaming presence
> the tangible star
> the crater's wine
> neither icon nor symbol nor cloud
> but more beautiful than icons
> more instructive than symbols
> more exhilarating than clouds
> more evasive and refreshing
> ("The Quarry," 62–70)

> tranquility is bestowed
> by the lightning presence
> which moves and resurrects all things

> anxiety is caused
> by the impending disappearance
> and all the grief
> which such libations abandon
> ("The Proclaimed," 22–28)

Images of blessing pass through the poems as unifying figures
too. The blooming thyme, an instrument of blessing, is carried
through "Faith and Hope" as expressive of the divine presence
which is the "spirit of the thyme" (39), and is recalled in a related image in "The Petrified Insect" where the miraculous hours
are described as "blessed with a moistened basil sprig" (16–17).
The beauties of creation in "The Attractions" are revealed as
"saturated / with your thyme's pungencies" (74–75), and in "Before a Journey," where man is preparing for a more spiritual
union with God, the physical sign of "that remnant thyme / now
dry" (113–114) becomes "the relic of a previous / foreign day"
(114–115).

Related to the religious imagery of blessing and the resurrection, images of blood tie the work together by their references
to Christ's blood, the blood of the classical furies, and the bloody
massacre of the war years in Greece: the bloodstained Erinys,
the dried-up cherry trees, the carnations which flare up in the
mouth as deep foam, the perfect "blood clot thickened in the

darkness / a clot which does not come alone" ("A Fearless Woman Dressed in Many Carnations," 104–105), the prickly pears and the blackberries that appear "so that thorns will tear us / to be bathed by blood" ("The Fates Lead," 3–4), and the stain which "was not blood and felt it/blemishes without shape" ("The Fates Lead," 44–45). This blood is not merely that of wounds; it is an image of divinity and the pain which must be experienced in coming to a God who in the voracious noons put to fire all things with his gigantic torch:

> the gaping noons
> consuming without being consumed
> kindled and kindling
> ("The Petrified Insect," 166–168)

The key image which expresses Papatsonis's cumulative and multiple vision of the blood, the carnation, and the fire of God occurs in "A Fearless Woman Dressed in Many Carnations":

> for besides their decorative graces
> they possessed the gift of fire
> their flame-red lips brusque Pentecostalisms
> purple crimson scarlet
> rose passionate speckled
> all frayings of a single sun
> (21–26)

In this image the major threads of the poem are brought together in a combination to be reflected again only in the final verses of the last poem of the whole work, a combination expressing the intense mystical interpenetration of pain and joy, of fire and light which attends the final revelation of God:

> for this revelation
> of the ethereal crimson we exhausted
> one long century
> all our hours' agonies
> at the observatory of such yearning
> and now that we have first seen the miracles
> to whom in haste and frenzy
> should we announce them but to you
> directress of the stars

helmsman of the sun which binds us
that you might hear it from our fury's riches

"from today love reigns" we tell you
"love reigns from today"
we shout it like marathon racers
having arrived hurriedly at life's threshold
but you disbelieve us
unfaithful implacable creation
and unaccustomed to revelations
we will thrust off your disbelief
because our announcements are true
etched with indisputable fire
be assured at last as we bring you the toil
of a squandered life
awaiting your acceptance of the knowledge
which this "reigns" conveys.

("The Attractions," 121–145)

VI   Recurrent Images

Among the symbols used throughout Papatsonis's poetry, those related to light, especially to the sun, recur more than any others. As an image the sun commonly occurs throughout modern Greek poetry, for, as Kimon Friar notes, modern Greek poets "have felt that in the dazzling sun of Greece the psychological dark labyrinths of the mind are penetrated and flooded with light, that in this merciless exposure one is led not to self-exploitation but to self-exploration under the glare of Necessity, that to 'Know Thyself' is for all Greeks, from ancient to modern times, the only preoccupation worthy of an individual. Beneath the blazing sun of Greece there is a sensuous acceptance of the body without remorse or guilt." [10]

In the works of some modern Greek writers—Elytis, Sikelianos, Kazantzakis, and Papatsonis—the sun is used as a symbol of some divine power beyond our physical grasp, a quality enhanced by the intensity and lucidity of the Greek sun. In the works of the Greek poets, the sun, according to Friar, is a "symbol of all that through intensity of natural fire and spiritual light impart an almost ethical meaning to the universe, a whitewash of cleansing sublimity, a purification of absolute noons." [11]

In Papatsonis's poetry this use of the sun can be seen in "I Sing the Wrath," 1941, a poem based on the poet's experiences during the Second World War. Reacting to the Italian invasion of his country through Albania, the poet calls on Pallas Athena, the patron goddess of Athens, to save the sun of Greece, for its essence is the essence of the nation itself:

> the Shield of the Virgin,
> the Shield which so protects the Sun of Greece
> that it may never alter or darken, may never be deprived,
> even in the slightest, of its ancient god-born Essence.
>   (54–57) °

"In A Summer Hour," 1928, refers again to the Greekness of Papatsonis's sun. He calls the "Miracle of the Sun" (4) the "Light of Greece or Apollonian Brilliance" (5). It is a fearsome sun which burns and terrorizes those who depend upon it for their heat. But it is also a wonder, something that must be understood:

> The Sun is in Leo, says the Almanac.
> How senseless. Fearing the
> lion would eat us,
> we were devoured roasted. Could the celestial master
>   of the flame
> have roared? I hear nothing.
> Could we have been taken for Blacks, shaped for furnaces?
> For this he was so inflamed. No, but as wayfarers
> lighting the fires of their camps at night
> saving themselves from beasts, so they mistook the Lion
> for a savage creature, and lit all of these hollow flames.
> Was it necessary? He is beautiful heavenly shapes,
> a loving enchantment in the nights, geometry in heaven's
>   canopy.
> He sought neither to rend us nor to roar.
> Then why so many fires without peril? Too much
> it seems celestial thoughts protect us.
> Might they not open a bit the box of winds,
> to blow upon us, to awake us from this narcotic life?
>   (37–52)

A reminder to man of the introspection that is necessary if he is to know himself, the sun in a later poem, "The Stone" (1929), keeps itself in one guise or another constantly before us:

> And even though
> but two or three hours ago it was preparing such a blazing

departure below and beyond the world, with trumpet
    blasts and crimson mantles,
and though hidden out of sight, it always knows how
    to send
something to remind us of its eternal presence.

Something secret during these hours is being weighed
    in the vitals of man,
and which, either as the Sun or the Moon, has enthroned
    itself
in the soul's midst, and grants him
the luminosity of a darkness that does not vary
from the mind of God or the contrition of the Church.
                         (15–24) °

In another aspect, the sun in "Incorruptibility" (1923) represents to the poet, possessed by his desire to achieve a weightless
soul, a means of resurrection:

Let me sit and compose myself,
to see the intrigues, the Sun old as time,
the Progress of the slow-mover amidst the prophetic
Shapes of the Clouds, to reach the Zenith,
and to shout "Set up the light, a wise
man is being resurrected; he once-dead in the Ravines,
in the Dusk, in the foliage, let him now rise with
the accompaniments of birds, warbling, watery streams
    and all the Joys
of a new Century."
        (17–25)

Again in "Redemption," 1933, the sun is the poet's means of
liberation:

                    Source of Light;
the counterpoise in the creation of the far wilderness,
momentarily installed, but at the same time Liberation
    from the Priest.
the suddenness of shameful Sin
in an hour of Redemption, is fixed.
           (20–24)

With Papatsonis, as with Sikelianos, the use of the sun as a
symbol stems not only from the power of the star itself, or from

his sense of it as a natural symbol, but also from his close reading of Dante. In both *Ursa Minor* and the *Commedia*, the sun is used to emphasize the increase in light as man nears the presence of God. In addition, however, a distinction between a physical and a spiritual sun as expressed in Plato's *Republic* is maintained in both the poems. Plato explains that in order to view an object, three factors are necessary: one who views, an object to be viewed, and light. He goes on to argue that a parallel occurs here between the use of vision and that of reason, for which a third factor is required. The Good is necessary as a mediator between reason itself and its object; it is the sun or light in the realm of ideas.

According to Plato, the sun not only grants to "visibles the power of visibility" (509B),[12] but also provides for their growth and nurturing. In the same manner objects of knowledge not only receive from the Good the ability to be known and understood, but also their very existence. The Good is both the cause of knowledge and truth and higher than these, just as the sun is both a part of light and vision and a higher property. As Anthony Joseph Mazzeo notes concerning Dante's *Commedia*, "There are thus two powers, the Good which reigns over the intelligible world and the sun which rules over the visible world. The one confers being on its world, the other is the principle of generation in its world." [13] Ultimately, however, both the Good and the sun are part of one power, that power which is known as God.

The distinction between a physical and a spiritual sun is maintained in *Ursa Minor*. Throughout the work one is reminded that light is necessary to distinguish the beauty of those objects which reflect the glory of God. Thus man, gazing at the beauty of the growing flowers under the spring sun, in "A Fearless Woman Dressed in Many Carnations" (21–26), is reminded of the Creator. The carnations of the spring are endowed not only with their "decorative graces," making them "purple crimson scarlet / rose passionate speckled" (21; 24–25), but with "the gift of fire" (22), the presence of the spiritual light of God which is visible in its physical manifestation. The carnations seem to speak with "flame-red lips" (23) to tell man of "brusque Pentecostalisms" (23), of things beyond his world. Similarly man harbors in his memory an idea of the Creator, of his source. The carnations are "all frayings of a single sun" (26); they are part of that which is the source of all light since they too shine with the light of the Eternal Sun. It is thus His light that acts as a mediary between man and the object being viewed and which is necessary to man's perception and understanding of Him.

Occupied with the temporal world, man lacks the light necessary to lead him to the true reality of things. As the poet says in "A Fearless Woman Dressed in Many Carnations," "for this the sharpness of our vision / has dulled so greatly" (121–122). It is the physical light emanating from the spiritual light that shows man the way to truth and the final realization of the Godhead: "Lit ashes fell on our eyes / and we saw the light" ("The Attractions," 1–2). It is when the ashes as mediators between man and God fall from the "torsions and nebulae" ("The Attractions," 3–4), from the lesser suns found in the heavens, that man "sees" the light which is the truth, the understanding of God.

That the physical sun encompasses more than man realizes, as Virgil states in *Purgatorio* XIII, is made clear in "The Petrified Insect." Here the hours are described as parts of the sun, for they form "the Olympian perfection / of a sun-born love" (22–23). All time, all eternity constitutes the perfection of God, that love which is the sun. The sun here is more than the physical sun which provides man with light to see. It is itself the source of that physical light, God himself.

In the last poem, "The Attractions," the sun is described as the source of all the other suns, planets and stars, the source from which they feed their flames: "you modestly nurture all the suns / perpetuate their flames" (44–45). The sun is here the director of all things and the power which balances the planets (48–49). It is only in the closing lines of *Ursa Minor* that the sun is seen as that which man has been seeking and finally finds. The sun is God, He who is to be reached only by means of the light of the physical sun which He sends to guide man to Him.

Transposing the classical influence into a Christian one, Papatsonis emphasizes noon as the hour of the day best fitted for man's ascendance to heaven, the hour when the sun is at its height and when Christ is said to have died and to have ascended. It is at the height of noon that Papatsonis introduces the "great glowing hours" ("The Petrified Insect," 161) when the presence of the soul is before one. The dark night of meditation is supplanted by "the voracious noons" ("The Petrified Insect," 163) when everything in the universe is set on fire, a fire lit by God Himself. It is at noon that the poet sits under a tree with the gold of the sun's rays streaming upon him "experiencing our sacred examination" ("The Petrified Insect," 178–179), a rite comparable in its purifying powers to Dante's drinking from the Eunoe. As Dante explains in the *Convito*, "the hour of noon is the noblest in the whole day and the one of greatest virtue." [14] Noon in Papatsonis, as in Dante, is the hour when one finds oneself in the presence of God, when man himself ascends to journey with the fire of noon, God Himself:

> this fire was our life's
> source and with it now
> we journey together
> ("The Petrified Insect," 184–186)

As *Ursa Minor* is a poem of a quest, the object of which lies in the heavens, its light imagery emanates not only from the sun but from the stars. The stars are the visible light of God's spiritual light which attracts and guides man toward the heavens. In "The Quarry" the stars are the reward for those who struggle to know God. They are the divine light that shines once man finds his faith, for once he believes in God, he will inherit "a night sky / filled with stars" (115–116). In "The Proclaimed" the "oscillations of the most distant stars" (67–68) enrich man, for they bring the spiritual light of God. In "The Petrified Insect" the stars "hurl their rays" (36) to guide him to the heavens, and Kallisto the beloved becomes the "star of paradise" (99).

As a counterbalance to the light imagery of Papatsonis's poetry, images of war and the language of war infuse his work, creating a picture of a misery-ridden world lacking in God's light, a world of darkness and without hope. In "Gigantes Gog et Magog," 1921, the poet turns to Revelations and retells the tale of the two giants, one from the north, the other from the south, who in the absence of the presence of God join in the darkness of battle over the earth:

> Under the two Giants' feet
> Cities tremble in their Midnight agony;
> terror-stricken souls, wretched ones, tremble
> within closed shutters.

How will it ever dawn? It will never dawn.
At one stroke earth's light was extinguished;
and the otherwise calm spheres of the stars, along with
distant familiar night tremors, were extinguished.
The two giants, fortresses of darkness, Gog and Magog.
In the district of the Wild Night they await in ambush
all the earthly Sphere, enemies to each other
and enemies of the Earth.
(9–20)

The deadly hate of this early poem is that of man's "inevitable Hell" in which God is only a memory. The world itself is the victim of dread forces which rage at will within it and which cut off its light.

Papatsonis's darkness is not, however, restricted to the biblical darkness of Daniel's battle with the lions in "Daniel in Fovea Leonum Signata" (1921), or to the war between the giants, Gog and Magog; it is extended to include the tragic darkness of real wars in the poet's own times. Using Homeric images to castigate the Italians who invaded Greece in World War II, "I Sing the Wrath" expresses the poet's response to what he considers both a personal and a national tragedy:

For their Agamemnon and Achilles and Ajax they chose
the most barbarously named Visconti and Ubaldo
and Caballero; the elegant Galeazzo also arrived,
and the Middle Ages and the Albanians were blackened
with shameful deeds, of which the Illyrians would
        have blushed to hear.
The Archipelago was blackened with the infamies of
        the abductors,
and they begged iron loans from the Teutons with which
to burn down, to turn into ash, the land of their
        envy, Greece.
        (32–39) *

Again darkness is associated with sin and is attributed to those who, in hate and greed, imitate jealous gods by igniting with fire the land of their envy.

In "A Fearless Woman Dressed in Many Carnations" the poet continues to treat his personal horror at the ravages of war, but in a more intense and deeply emotional way:

[120]

> where are they now discarded
> where might they be viewed decomposed
> these sad downtrodden bodies
> which lost their wounds
> and gained the root and earth
> (50–54)

Papatsonis's image depicts "sad bodies" discarded like withered flowers, bodies treated as objects which have served their purpose and have been left to decompose, to become once again part of "the root and earth." Papatsonis speaks further of the "unjust pains the hushed screams" ("A Fearless Woman Dressed in Many Carnations," 64) of torture victims, recalling the tortures inflicted upon the Greeks by the Nazis: "the steel that whitens the dawn of day / the tuft of smoke" ("A Fearless Woman Dressed in Many Carnations," 71–72). Referring specifically to a rifle barrel and the aftermath of a shot, the image in its most extended sense is a reminder, as the poet explains, of cremating furnaces and the last evidence of inhuman acts, a signal to waiting relatives that their worst fears have been confirmed.

At times dying men are described as petals falling from flowers:

> now they are being severed
> not the flowers' petals any longer
> but men themselves
> ("A Fearless Woman Dressed in
> Many Carnations," 91–93)

Elsewhere the poet describes the "dissatisfied wandering breath" ("A Fearless Woman Dressed in Many Carnations," 41) of death as a scented cloud and the

> equal numbered wounds either lively or faded
> mournful calm or agitated
> their suffering always enclosed in the cup
> in multiple curves and arcs
> in bends and painful trajectories
> ("A Fearless Woman Dressed in
> Many Carnations," 31–35)

Deeply touched by the loss of human life that occurred in Greece during the war, Papatsonis was sensitized to the brutality of which man is capable. His poem "The Lamentation of a Greek for the Martyrdom and the Condemnation of Joseph Mindzenty," 1949, eloquently expresses his despair at the trials which the innocent must suffer:

> And as the holidays approached and as the bells struck,
> he, the great bishop, dressed in his gold garments
> and in roses
> would walk in the processional
> from the church of Saint Mathew, holding the Holy Chalice,
> and all the faithful would rush and kneel before him
> like a swelling wave that they might receive
> in his passing the eminent blessing.
>
> They have locked the bishop now in a dungeon.
>
> Not since the Ottomans threatened the iron gates
> had such a shame, such calamity occurred.
> Such sufferings had been put to rest for years, epochs.
> You would think that men had been pacified. I don't
> remember
> when I learned how the unrighteous with such beastiality
> sat the innocent on the seat of judgment.
> The papers write, "For eighty hours
> they questioned him, without rest, standing upright."
> They sucked his will. They set themselves
> to uproot his soul together with the triple crown.
> "Today the just lion is deposited in a sealed cave
> that he might shed
> before he dies a debt he does not owe."
> (37–59)

In spite of the sufferings Mindzenty underwent, he is depicted by the poet as ever constant in the purity of his soul, inspiring others to retain their faith:

> Do you not see him, like a child, seeking
> the blessing you have cut off with your hammerings?
> And do you not see his soul, that of all the people,
> coiled like a rose
> under his moldy crust,
> gushing up, a clot of pulsing blood
> concealing itself within the bars of the jail,

in order to kiss the hand
decorated with a multicolored stone, the hand of love?
(76–84)

The poet becomes increasingly conscious, beyond all the darkness and horrors of war and human cruelty, of the necessity of a
return to the universal brotherhood of man. In this poem, beyond
all else he has written, Papatsonis is brought to a culminating
realization of the nature of suffering in all lands:

But, you will say, of what concern to you is that
which happens in a foreign land? I will explain:
elegies for all have been composed,
the first, for the loss of Velouchioti,
the second for the indissoluble gloom of Andalusia,
for Ignatio Mexia, the bullfighter,
the third, for the unjustly shortened youth
of a hypothetical engaged lieutenant,
the fourth for the frigate sunk by a cannonball
which rots in a far-off corner of the ocean,
the fifth, a dithyramb for a double-natured
scattered hero of Greece and of Venezuela
in the same way my heart moves me to lament
today in my own manner, a convict archbishop.
But, you will say, what do you care for a foreigner?
Have men become so foreign among themselves,
so foreign that the bitter unanimous lamentation
of a nation, which whip and mockery have befallen,
will not rend our heart at all?
And is their lamentation, in truth, so foreign,
since the same blood's mantle
and the blood-red river have surrounded me?
Is this blood which belts our mountains
and stains their snows different? The wind carries
as far as our city smoke from the scorching
of their olive trees which their burning left behind.
And a great shout is heard in Rama, close to me,
grieving and wailing for the children.
(85–112)

VII *Conclusion*

Papatsonis's style is characterized by the metaphysical imagery
which infuses his poetry, an imagery which appears to flow freely

from the subconscious in a great outpouring of feeling. Appearing often arbitrarily juxtaposed and contextually disjointed, his individual images combine the visual and concrete with the surreal-like and mystical in a pleasurable exoticism which is at times dreamlike, at other times painterly in its details, and at yet other times mosaic- or puzzlelike. His most widely used device, the concretization of the abstract, is used typically to clothe the immaterial in sensual attributes which give it shape and dimension.

Papatsonis is a poet whose largest concern is with the highly personal faith and vision of his poetry. Substance dominates over the loose form of his work as he transforms his mythic materials, both pagan and Christian, into a philosophy which is both deductively proselike and lyrically mystical. Rhythmically and metrically simple, his work can be complex in its imagery, invoking in its peculiar mixture of the erotic, the esoteric, and the ecstatic an exquisitely refined sense of the religious.

Chapter 5

Religious Views and Influences

PAPATSONIS, in a personal interview of June 2, 1969, indicated that he prefers to view his poetic output as basically "pantheist," rather than "religious." Cleon Paraschos, too, emphasizes the pantheism in Papatsonis's poetry in his essay "The Poetry of Takis Papatsonis." "All of his symbols," he says, "necessarily refer to the One, for in all things Papatsonis confronts, beholds, and senses the presence of the One. . . ." [1] Panayiotis Kanellopoulos, the Greek statesman and man of letters, in praising Papatsonis's language, refers to him as a "noble and graceful, religious nature who finds God in the vast creation, in beautiful nature and in the heart of true humanity." [2]

Everything in the universe reveals God in the poetry of Papatsonis, especially in *Ursa Minor*. In "Faith and Hope" all things are shown to reveal the Creator, from the sun, the sea, the planets, down to "the pine's caress" (7) and "the unsullied hard sky's reflections" (5). In "The Petrified Insect" everything vibrates around God, the source of life, (1–4); indeed, every hour that exists brings out His grandeur:

> hours of flowers which accept
> the water we offer
> hours of flowers
> when they are saddened
> and they begrudge us
> hours of reflected
> worship annihilated
> by the single-edged scythe
> ears of corn overgrown
> their gathering
> hours sulphurized
> by eccentricities and the inclinations
> of heaven's musk tree

> which dawns and dies
> as though we did not exist
>
> sea-beaten hours
> hours of the wind
> hours of clouds
> portraying your great beauty
> and the labyrinths of your moods
> but they lack in the multiplicity of forms
> and the Daedalean depth
> (79–92)

As in Ecclesiastes 3, there is a time for the sea, the wind, the clouds, a time for all creation that depicts the great beauty of which the soul is but a part. The varied parts of the universe demonstrate the incomprehensibility of Him who created them and, as in "The Attractions," draw us by the love they express, a love that pervades all the universe, that resides in all things, both good and bad. But we are unable to endure the dichotomy of a universe in which God must appear to us as both destructive and constructive and are confused by the contradictory aspects of this highest divinity:

> you cleave our heart
> designating it your hearth
> without ever accepting
> its hospitality
> with but a single sign you activate
> the yawning craters
> in the menace of our black mountain
> you unfold fully green vineyards
> near the sea
> on the sulphurized slopes of lava
> like thickset armies you congregate
> the lemon trees on the plain
> and we cannot endure this double drunkenness
> as you send it tempered
> with your disposition's pungencies
> in a potion which until now
> we discerned as death's
> our autonomy is in fragments
> and these glitter as you rattle them
> with the sword of your flame
> (61–80)

God is here shown in his double nature both in activating vol-
canoes and in spreading green fields; he brings forth armies of
lemon trees on the "sulphurized slopes of lava." Believing that to
be evil from which good arises, man sees the "double drunken-
ness" of creation as unendurable.

Man's soul is itself but a shell in which resides the presence
of God, a presence to be found even in the smallest objects in
nature which both contain and reveal him. The flowers of "A
Fearless Woman Dressed in Many Carnations" with their "flame-
red lips" (23) are merely "frayings of a single sun" (126). They
are but fragments of a greater whole which attracts and governs
all. In "The Attractions" even the "negligible dust" (3) which
descends from the universe is a revealer of the Divine and contains part of His divinity. A "drop of milk" (5) from the galaxy
fills man with the expectation of that love of which it is a part,
indicating yet again that all parts of the universe reveal God, for
they are all part of Him.

Papatsonis's vision of universal oneness is essentially, though not
explicitly, that expressed by Plotinus in *Ennead* IV.4.3: "The soul
is many things, is all, is the Above and the Beneath to the totality
of life: and each of us is an Intellectual Cosmos, linked to the
world by what is lowest in us, but by what is the highest, to the
Divine Intellect: by all that is intellective we are permanently in
that higher realm but at the fringe of the Intellectual we are
fettered to the lower; it is as if we gave forth from it some emana-
tion towards that lower, or rather some Act which however leaves
our diviner part not in itself diminished." [3] For Papatsonis, the
soul is most securely tied to its lower manifestations in moments of
weakness and sin. Cast into the terrors of war in *Ursa Minor*, man
is isolated from the higher realm of intellect that represents
beauty and love to the poet. It is only when man learns to accept
his place as part of everything in nature and to submit to God
as love that he will be reintegrated into the "totality of life" that
leads like links of a chain to the Divinity.

But such a path, for self-conscious man, is not one which he
can travel with ease, certainly not with the ease of natural phenomena such as time in "The Petrified Insect" which, unen-
cumbered, reveals "the Olympian perfection / of a sunborn love"
(22–23) as a reflection of His order and symmetry. Recognizing
man's agitation, nature does not, however, forsake him, but

demonstrates her active sympathy for his inability to reconcile his existence with the world in which he lives, his inability to perceive all things as belonging to one whole:

> mint lavender
> and rosemary all
> pray for us all however
> love us all
> collect about us
> their sympathy and concern
> espying our uneasiness
> rising in heaps hiding
> indifference
> perceiving us bound
> by agitation not at all
> eclipsed by all the warbling of our exaltation
> and even that remnant thyme
> now dry the relic of a previous
> foreign day in every way
> attempts to show us
> it is with us in this strenuous
> trial and thus let us all
> the travelers of the moment say
> that we found ourselves strongly bound
> ("Before A Journey," 101–120)

As Plotinus states in the *Enneads*, "Things here are signs: they show therefore to the wiser teachers how the supreme God is known; the instructed priest reading the sign may enter the holy place and make real the vision of the inaccessible" (VI.9.11).

In moments of despair, picturing the dark abyss before him, man may halt, but ultimately presses on toward the light. As Papatsonis says in "Faith and Hope,"

> but that which we longed for
> was not here at all
> in such a slithery tar-paved abyss
> and this all-powerful desire's
> supreme effort
> "the one who dared such things"
> always so miraculous
> we did not wish such an abyss
> to swallow
> (73–81)

This "all-powerful" desire, union with God, is a voice within us that tells us we are a part of creation and the Creator. This faith of ours for which we risk our lives is miraculous, something unborn which man does not wish to have swallowed up in the abyss. The poet believes that despair can be conquered and man must have the faith and the stamina to pursue his search for God, a search in which, for both Papatsonis and Plotinus, the universe is a revealer of God's majesty and love that constantly draws man toward the heavens. In *Ursa Minor* this love attracts like a magnet and invites us to become one with it ("The Attractions," 37–41). It is an attraction which, as explained in "The Proclaimed," cannot be rejected, but which eternally draws us out of our abyss:

> this Attraction
> never to be acknowledged
> by renouncement
> dwells in eternity
> an attraction of space
> the best omen of our resistance
> the nailing and embrace
> the reward of which without this
> would be the abyss
> our luminescence
> the symmetry
> the justification and sanctification
> of our most obstinate fatalism
> (139–151)

It is the Plotinian "appetite for the divine Intellect" (*Ennead* IV.8.4) which urges the soul to return to its source: "all that exists desires and aspires towards the Supreme by a compulsion of nature, as if all had received the oracle that without it they cannot be" (*Ennead* V.5.12).

This attraction is constant for it is a law of the universe and, as Papatsonis says, this "law is the mightiest" ("The Proclaimed," 136) for it keeps "in motion the now transported firmament" ("Faith and Hope," 48), it maintains the "great equilibrious harmony" ("The Proclaimed," 5). Without its symmetry there "would be the abyss" ("The Proclaimed," 147), darkness and chaos, "all things will remain immobile / without their tractions or expansions' ("Faith and Hope," 54–55), the grass will not grow ("The Proclaimed," 121), nor flowers bloom ("The Proclaimed," 123), the winds and the ripples on the sea will no longer have any impetus ("The Proclaimed," 124–126).

The order in the Plotinian universe (*Ennead* I.6.2, 6; III.6.3, 4; V.5.9; V.8.2, 3) is an order of love; everything operates under the force of love which "has of necessity been eternally in existence, for it springs from the intention of the Soul towards its Best, towards the Good; as long as Soul has been, Love has been" (*Ennead* III.5.9). Plotinus's order is that of the Good toward which all things strive through love which "stirs and leads upwards the souls of the young and every soul with which it is incorporated in so far as there is a natural tendency to remembrance of the divine. For every soul is striving toward the Good, even the mingling Soul and that of particular beings, for each holds directly from the divine Soul and is its offspring" (*Ennead* III.5.3).

In *Ursa Minor* the force that directs the stars and balances the planets, the force that is order and harmony itself ("The Attractions," 48–49), is personalized in "the panarchaic queen of love" ("The Attractions," 101), Aphrodite. This love gives of itself to all other created things in the universe so that all things are merely reflections of it. In "The Attractions" this force—which is God, the sun, and love—feeds "all the suns" (44); it is the source of all light, for the stars and planets merely reflect the light of the major sun, which is the light of love. It is this love that "perpetuates their flames" (45), a concept expressed by Plotinus in *Ennead* I. 1.8: "The soul appears to be present in the bodies by the fact that it shines into them: it makes them living beings not by merging into body but by giving forth, without any change in itself, images or likenesses of itself like one face caught by many mirrors."

Papatsonis's view of love is thus in many ways comparable to that of Plotinus, a debt which Papatsonis himself freely admits in a letter to the present author, dated January 7, 1972: "What I have in common with Plotinus's philosophy is the firm belief that our soul is a parcel of the universe, and as such immortal. The existence of this link proves the divine part of our substance and gives strength and patience against miseries and misfortunes to individuals who believe in this doctrine during the period of our earthly and perishable life." In this sense, what man hoped to teach his body is that it will finally set; that as it dies, only the light of the soul, the essential part of man's nature, will remain, and the purified soul, having nothing to weigh it down, will ascend naturally back to its source.

II *Mysticism*

Papatsonis's mysticism was recognized early in his poetry by a number of Greek critics. Paraschos wrote in 1947: "In Papatsonis this feeling for mysticism, evident even in his early poetry, has grown richer and stronger, has reached new heights and is becoming organized (if one may use such a word about something so fluid) into a permanent fixed religious attitude which permeates, penetrates, and colors all his work." [4] Papatsonis has been called a "Christian mystic," [5] a mystic of nature, [6] a Neo-Hellenic mystic, [7] and as early as 1916 was referred to by Kostis Palamas, modern Greece's dean of letters and one of her greatest poets, as a mystic who "suffers from the love of God. . . ." [8] The poet himself has alluded to his mysticism in his essay "Myth and History," which deals with similarities between his own poetry and that of George Seferis: "Parallel with these dry influences, however, much stronger remained the esoteric psychic stream which, during the passing of sad and worthy years, every now and then would make itself known and explain the multiple union which united me with Seferis." [9]

Infused with the light of both Dante and Plotinus, Papatsonis's work has much in common with yet a third mystic, St. John of the Cross. As the poet specifies in the essay on Seferis, any list of influences on his work would have to contain "at the head of all the Bible, Dante—and for me St. John of the Cross." [10] Preoccupied with the darkness of man's journey through life, Papatsonis's quest throughout his poetry has been to find the light of God. As St. John of the Cross wrote in *Letters* I: "To suffer darkness is the way to great light. The soul draws nearer and nearer to the divine union in darkness. If the soul will see, he thereby becomes instantly more blind as to God than he who should attempt to gaze upon the sun shining in its strength." [11] It is during such a dark night of the soul as St. John demonstrates in *"Dark Night of the Soul* II.5 that "God secretly teaches the soul and instructs her in the perfection of love, without efforts on her own part beyond a loving attention to God, listening to His voice and admitting the light He sends."

In *Ursa Minor* Papatsonis, too, waits for the evening to contemplate God. In "Faith and Hope" it is evening which comes forth "with its own honey tones/with its own crispness and flux" (12–13) and brings the poet peace of mind from the cares of the day. When the stars appear in the sky, every care dissolves into the darkness (18–22), and the heavens, opening, reveal the light of God (30–40). Thus in *Ursa Minor* the divine is contemplated in the darkness of the night until the poet is finally able to transcend his material boundaries and give himself over completely to God. At that point night no longer prevails and all becomes light. The poet then finds himself sitting under a tree at the height of noon contemplating God, but careful not to look straight into the sun lest he be blinded by its power ("The Petrified Insect," 170–183). St. John of the Cross speaks of such noons in *Spiritual Canticle of the Soul* I as "the midday which is Eternity, where the Father is ever begetting and the Son ever begotten." Edmund G. Gardner, speaking of the mysticism in the *Commedia* in his work *Dante and the Mystics,* remarks that "noon has a special significance for the mystics, as representing celestial desire, or divine illumination, or eternity." [12]

Papatsonis's mysticism is perhaps nowhere else in the poet's work expressed so intensely as it is in *Ursa Minor,* where it takes the form of a sensual, pain-ridden ecstasy. It is a mysticism of love such as Gardner describes in speaking of Dante: "Love is thus the guide of mysticism from the start to the goal, and love is its beginning and its end. Love leads the mystics, in their search for absolute truth and absolute beauty, to a state in which for a moment . . . the soul is permeated with the Divine. We might define Mysticism as the love-illumined quest of the soul to unite herself with the suprasensible—with the absolute—with that which is." [13]

This "love-illumined quest of the soul to unite herself with the suprasensible" is eloquently expressed in "The Petrified Insect" where, in the final image of the poem, the scarab, representing the soul or God, becomes

> the image of the merciless cannonball
> which impregnates love
> the icon of creation
> as it pulsates

> in the passion of its ignition
> (222–226)

The "cannonball" is God's mercy which enters and fills us with love, an experience both painful and sensual. It is this primal and initiating act of love which brings life to the soul in the same way that man fills woman with child; in this act of passion which ignites the pulse of life, the icon of creation consumes and replenishes itself throughout eternity. This same sensuality is evident in "The Attractions" in the image of the moon appearing after the end of day: "for the first time the hidden one appears to us / who until yesterday was still in the arms of day" (97–98). Here the moon, Artemis "the hidden one" who is denied us by day, is immersed in a sensual embrace in which day and the moon merge into one.

The conveyance of the mystic attitude, of the ecstasy, pain, and sensuality of the mystic experience, is most typically in Papatsonis's poetry expressed through concrete images. In "The Proclaimed" one finds the poet gazing into the heavens in the evening, in a state of ecstasy contemplating God. Secure in the presence of God, he lies in ecstasy confronting love:

> it is tranquility matched
> to the durability of the excitement
> it is security enthroned
> in a bed of gushing fever
> (17–20)

The poet here is like the lover waiting for the coming of the loved one, Kallisto. At times, as in "The Petrified Insect," the wind both caresses as a lover and inflicts its strength as man ("Before a Journey," 5–8). At other times as the poet contemplates love, he sees the heavens spread before him:

> all concealed voluptuosness
> dauntlessly spread
> lavishly courageous
> ("The Petrified Insect," 25–27)

At such times all the voluptuosness of the universe lies spread before him with much of the sensuality and secrecy of a passionate woman offering herself.

[133]

In lines 127–147 of the same poem, the poet is concerned with man's yearning for God, his soul. The image Papatsonis presents is again one of a lover yearning for his beloved, counting and re-counting the hours of her absence, longing for her:

> and we count them the uncountable
> and number them
> the innumerable
> now on one accent
> then on the other
> occasionally triumphantly
> with a shout of joy
> often with lamentation
> at times with the heart's
> dry wringing
> sometimes with the frenzied bitterness
> of your absence's hyoscyamine
> (127–138)

Together with such sensuality, there occurs throughout *Ursa Minor* a constant emphasis on the pain experienced in combination with such intense love. In "The Attractions" we feel touched and drawn by the power of love (61–72) which informs the universe; we long to become part of it. When we finally join with it, however, we lose our independence and become fragments joined with other fragments of the universe, shining as part of the domain of the sun:

> our autonomy is in fragments
> and these glitter as you rattle them
> with the sword of your flame
> (78–80)

The image of union with God, as elsewhere in *Ursa Minor*, is expressed in terms of pain and suffering, for we are like slaves shattered by the flaming sword of our master, an image continued in the following verse where the sword is identified with the sun and love:

> the great magnet of the world
> the glinting steel

which draws and kills
(81–83)

The sword is seen as the great magnet that attracts us to the heavens. Once, however, we have reached the spiritual state, we leave behind us our material world. Thus, the "glinting steel," the sword of the previous verse and, again, a sexual image, attracts and makes us part of the Oneness, though it also "kills," both in destroying our material selves and in the sense of consummation of the sexual act.

Elsewhere in *Ursa Minor*, Kallisto the beloved is described in terms of painful love. She is described by "those crooked nails of barren love" ("The Petrified Insect," 102–103) we feel in our flesh, and the "sudden blaze" ("The Petrified Insect," 190) we feel in our hearts at her coming. When she arrives to guide us toward God "we receive her fiery sword strokes / on our hearts and are inflamed" ("The Proclaimed," 31–32), as a wound both painful and sweet, one welcomed by the poet on the path to God. Even the thorns of a rose ("The Fates Lead," 27) are desirable, for the pains of true beauty, the beauty of Kallisto, are welcome pains. Like the thorns, the poet's thoughts of God lead him painfully along his journey:

> then as the birds'
> bills aggravate
> the bleeding
> open wounds
> of our doubts
> ("The Petrified Insect," 52–56)

The birds peck at the poet's open doubts, much in the manner of the eagle of Zeus plucking at the gaping wound of Prometheus. They are the poet's thoughts of God that will soon soar upward toward the heavens and return with greater understanding of the Divine. But such thoughts are painful, for they invoke the wounds of our doubts as we make a choice between our material and spiritual worlds.

III *Journey*

The mysticism and pantheism which color Papatsonis's poetry express the poet's search for God as he journeys in meditation

through the heavens toward unity with the Creator. In Papatsonis's Christian view this journey is, as he explains in a letter
dated June 25, 1968, one which has conditioned all his work:
"Everything I have written could be considered as a mere contemplative diary of my soul's process in the continuous endeavour
to acquire a union with the Cosmos, the unknown forces governing the universe. A mystic element, I dare say, has persisted in
my work in an attempt (imperfect as all human attempts are) to
approach the idea of God."

Papatsonis's journey throughout his poetry is influenced to a
large extent by Dante's journey in the *Commedia,* and nowhere
more explicitly than in the former's *Ursa Minor.* The *Ursa Minor's*
opening parallels the *Commedia,* for it opens in a dark and om-
inous world with fear and faithlessness lurking everywhere. The
poet finds himself in a world of "the uncompassionate darkness /
the miserable vertigo of cowardice" ("A Fearless Woman Dressed
in Many Carnations," 68–69). It is in such despair that his call for
divine aid, like Dante's to Beatrice, is heard by Kallisto, the guide
of men and their only hope for salvation:

> thanks to you they have now found their icon
> their glory and their worship
> their refuge
> found at least a gaudy requiem
> in their own reddening
> > ("A Fearless Woman Dressed in
> > Many Carnations," 78–82)

It is in Kallisto that the poet and all those suffering on earth find
an image of worship that their suffering may embrace.

In "Faith and Hope" Papatsonis speaks of man's fall into sin at
the loss of faith. Initially, as the poet gazes at the polar star in
the evening sky, his heart fills with peace. The evening reveals to
him God's beauty, bringing Kallisto's constellation into view
"united to [God's] perpetual happiness" ("Faith and Hope," 35–
36). But Kallisto is too distant. Her absence, like Beatrice's absence from Dante (*Purgatorio* XXXI.34–36), takes the poet's
mind from God, and without the faith that she represents the
poet despairs:

> What remains we abhor most
> reverie and poverty in your absence the compromises

and now finally that which spread
as a great black blot of secret fear
an immense crow's wing
terror of the eventual

("Faith and Hope," 41–46)

In Kallisto's absence the poet is made poorer and must compromise with life and the material world; what remains is "an immense crow's wing," the overhanging darkness of despair that attends the loss of her brilliance:

the despairing night will last forever
strength and courage will be exhausted
in sterile painted expectation
while all things will remain immobile
without their tractions or expansions
and our life once found
on the picturesque border of a well
so near alongside her happiness
while hand in hand we danced
with cheerful Grace
abruptly the hand was orphaned
and neglected a blind man's extended arm
seeking direction but losing it
there within the all-encompassing darkness
of the abyss which this evening has
nothing to illuminate

("Faith and Hope," 51–66)

Kallisto has "orphaned" the poet's hand, leaving it to reach without direction, without the guiding light of her constellation in "the abyss which this evening has / nothing to illuminate." The poet pictures the heavens transformed in the darkness of war and in the despair of man's loss of faith which renders all the universe immobile.

The poet, however, is determined to find his lost faith once again:

for whatever came with the moment's
squalls to recede from us
we cry out with faith that soon
we will find it again
reinhabit it

we will become its sun
("Faith and Hope," 82–87)

He is determined to make the journey to Kallisto in order to bring light and meaning to his faith. Crying out for union with his lost guide, he affirms they will form "the earth's new summer day" (90), a day which will arrive in "the year of our love" (92). It is through this union with faith that the poet believes man can find the image of God, the idol of beauty which, soulless and buried,

stirred at our coming
took life rekindled
remained beautiful touched us
and won us over
("Faith and Hope," 105–108)

The light of faith leads man to take up the path to God and is necessary to man's discovery of that love which is God. Man follows the path with bleeding feet to the place where lies the marble idol, an image of God's beauty which lies buried deep within man and which stirs and rekindles itself only as faith begins to awaken within man.

In "The Fates Lead" the poet completely regains the faith he had lost. The Fates who are to carry him to God appear to him as an "imposing army dressed in white" (115–116), coming from "the plain of white hope" (124), taking on the color of faith. It is these Fates dressed in white who "won for us at least / our hesitant resistance" (119–120); it is they who permit man to surmount the boundaries of the material world. Having renewed himself before the Fates who are to guide him to heaven, man is prepared to become an active questing agent, claiming

it is not even time
to regret inertness
or thoughtless torpidity
now that the fates lead
("The Fates Lead," 127–130)

In "The Petrified Insect" the poet is subjected to a "sacred examination" (179) of his faith at the height of "the great glowing hours" (161), the gaping and voracious noons. Like Dante before his three inquisitors (*Paradiso* XXIV, XXV, XXVI), the poet is brought before a divine judge and tested:

> there the first cicada
> only yesterday chirped
> and found us seated
> in a corner experiencing
> our sacred examination
> and the fire's sting
> at which we did not risk looking
> directly lest we go blind
> tyrannized us much
> ("The Petrified Insect," 175–183)

Having been led to faith by his guide and having submitted to a test of his faith, the poet can now "exhume" the soul, of whose existence he had become aware in poem two, from within the idol. But he is not yet prepared to completely understand the soul:

> the hard petrified insect
> does not reveal its secret
> as much as it is carved
> with scratches of worship
> the responsible magic stigma
> ("The Petrified Insect," 216–220)

In his preparation for a vision of the Creator as a reward of his faith, the poet is made ready in "The Attractions" through divine signs:

> lit ashes fell on our eyes
> and we saw the light
> silver dust emanated from the torsions
> and nebulae to adorn us
> a drop of milk
> fell on us from the milky way
> and pleased us
> water ran silently
> from Aquarius's Urns
> (1–9)

His eyes are annointed by ashes of stellar dust which fall on them, by "a drop of milk" from the galaxy, and by the pouring upon him of water "from Aquarius's Urns" which bathe him. The waters of purification which prepare man for God in *Ursa Minor* serve the same purpose as those of Lethe in which Dante was bathed (*Purgatorio* XXXI). Wholly restored in his faith and made pure in his hope, man may now journey to God, disencumbered of past sins and worthy of his Creator, to receive the miracles which are the fruit of Divine Grace.

Kallisto, the embodiment of the divine principle, may now be perceived in a second coming, descending to Arcadia in all her glory ("The Attractions," 15–36), and the poet, permitted a vision of love in its most intense form, is granted, like Dante (*Paradiso* XXXIII), a blinding view of God as light, God as the royal light of the "ethereal crimson" ("The Attractions," 125). He is led to a final recognition of God as love and the pervasive presence of that love in life:

> for this revelation
> of the ethereal crimson we exhausted
> one long century
> all our hours' agonies
> at the observatory of such yearning
> and now that we have first seen the miracles
> to whom in haste and frenzy
> should we announce them but to you
> directress of the stars
> helmsman of the sun which binds us
> that you might hear it from our fury's riches
>
> "from today love reigns" we tell you
> "love reigns from today"
> we shout it like marathon racers
> having arrived hurriedly at life's threshold
> but you disbelieve us
> unfaithful implacable creation
> and unaccustomed to revelations
> we will thrust off your disbelief
> because our announcements are true,
> etched with indisputable fire
> be assured at last as we bring you the toil
> of a squandered life
> awaiting your acceptance of the knowledge
> which this "reigns" conveys.
>
> ("The Attractions," 121–145)

The difference in manner between Papatsonis's handling of the journey and Dante's may be seen most clearly in the subtle and ever-changing treatment given Kallisto as a symbol of the soul. She is revealed initially as the fearless woman dressed in many carnations of the dedication: "you have the courage to dress / in carnations and I admire you" (56–57). At first an icon of the suffering of her people, she becomes

> the icon of a newly martyred legion
> of whatever would dissolve in the moistness of forgetfulness
> of whatever would evaporate to the five winds
> ("A Fearless Woman Dressed in Many Carnations," 61–63)

She is later revealed transformed by the horrors of war:

> for this you too remain a red icon
> wreathed in your many carnations
> immobile but ready and frightful
> my beloved Erinys
> the bloodstained
>
> (123–127)

But the roses with which she is also associated are those of the queen of love, the hidden one who establishes in us her sovereignty. In the final poem, "The Attractions," she is the sun passing through the signs of the zodiac (112–120), and she becomes the soul as the blinding sun in "The Petrified Insect," the brilliant God of fire who consumes those who would look upon Him in the brightness of His light (163–168; 180–189). She is at the same time "directress of the stars / helmsman of the sun which binds us" ("The Attractions," 129–130). It is she to whom men carry the final message of the miracle, crying out, "'from today love reigns' we tell you / 'love reigns from today'" ("The Attractions," 132–133), and hoping she will accept their understanding as genuine.

The soul expands in meaning to Papatsonis and is reflected in images widely divergent, suggestive of the multiple forms of life in a pantheistic universe. She is described as a lion, a tiger, a leopard ("The Quarry," 82–83); she is seen as a gleaming presence ("The Quarry," 63), as wine ("The Quarry," 65), as the coolness and secrecy of clouds ("The Quarry," 68–69); she is represented as "a merciless cannonball / which impregnates love" ("The Petrified Insect," 222–223), and she takes on the likeness of a lightning flash which slices across the heart with a fiery sword and leaves its wound ("The Proclaimed," 29–32).

In spite of their differences, however, Papatsonis borrowed from Dante his Christian themes, the framework of his poem, and his female guide to compose a work paralleling Dante's as a personal document written as a symbol of hope in a time of despair. Disillusioned at the time of the composition of their respective poems, both Dante and Papatsonis were in exile from their native states, Dante in physical exile from his war-torn Florence and Papatsonis in internal exile in brutally ravaged Greece. In both poems, however, there is expressed the hope that despair will be alleviated and that the world will be engulfed in a harmony of love.

Ursa Minor as a personal statement of a man suffering in a world corrupted by civil strife carries the reader well into the world of Dante's *Commedia.* It is a work whose fundamental view is based on the dehumanization of war in a period of hatred and strife and on love achieved through hope and faith, a view substantially influenced by Cantos XXIV, XXV, and XXVI of the *Paradiso,* which themselves treat the themes of faith, hope, and love. In these three cantos of *Paradiso,* Papatsonis discovered, as he indicates in his essay "A Triptych from Dante's Paradiso," a triad of values which, he believed, expressed the true purpose of the *Paradiso.* Treating cantos XXIV, XXV, and XXVI of the *Paradiso* as fundamental to Dante's Christian vision, Papatsonis borrowed just those three essential values—faith, hope, and love— from the *Commedia* as the base of his own *Ursa Minor.* The complexity of Dante's theological system is reduced to just those core elements which would express the purest form of Dante's vision.

Faith, seen by Dante as "the substance of what we hope to see / and the argument for what we have not seen" (*Paradiso* XXIV.64–65), has been lost to man in the opening of the *Commedia,* according to Papatsonis. Man thus hesitates in hope and is no longer assured of "the certain expectation / of future glory" (*Paradiso* XXV.66–67), the Dantean "blessed fruit / of grace divine and the good a man has done" (*Paradiso* XXV.67–68). Not until he has been made whole in his faith and complete in his hope, according to Papatsonis, can the poet proceed to the Essence (Perfection) toward which the mind gravitates once it has seen the truth which compels love (*Paradiso* XXVI.31–36). Only then can he receive the reward of faith, a vision of God.

In *Ursa Minor* Papatsonis focuses on the three theological virtues which he understood to be the core of Dante's *Paradiso* in an attempt to find a solution to the dilemma of modern man. Seeing about him a world in ruins and modern man in a desperate search for direction, Papatsonis took up in his *Ursa Minor* the Odyssean quest for his home. Unlike Seferis who concludes that the quest is fruitless, for modern man has been rendered homeless by his wars, Papatsonis turns to the Dantean journey, to another world, to find a truer home, to the indestructible home of the spirit. But Papatsonis's quest is a limited one designed to solve a particular and limited problem, while Dante's journey, as Curtius states in his *European Literature and the Latin Middle Ages*, was one in which "the entire cosmos of history is unfolded, to be apportioned anew in the astrophysical cosmos of the structure of the world and in the metaphysical cosmos of the transcendant. Physical cosmology and the metaphysical realm of values are interconnected in the strictest correlation." [14]

Dante's task was one which encompassed the whole cultural history of the Latin Middle Ages and antiquity. As a modern poet some distance in time from the classical tradition of both the Latin and Hellenic cultures, Papatsonis's vision is less encompassing than Dante's. He borrows only select themes from the classical past, themes which can be considered parallel to those with which the poet is concerned in contemporary culture. His use of the Byzantine Greek language is largely atmospheric, a recognition of the continuity of a generalized theology from the Byzantine past to present-day Greece. Nowhere does Papatsonis exhibit the wide knowledge of theological concepts and of specific canonical lore that is present in the *Commedia*, nor does he reflect a cosmological vision of the same definition and complexity as that which appears in Dante's highly incorporative poem.

The inferno, purgatory, and paradise are treated in *Ursa Minor* as dreamlike realms which have none of the structure with which they are imbued in the *Commedia*. Both the abyss of agony that constitutes Papatsonis's earthly existence and the heavenly ecstasy of his spiritual existence are amorphous states treated by the poet as highly personal inner experiences, whereas Dante preserves a quality of objectivity in his journey and maintains a sense of well-defined reality even in the heavenly realm. As Erich Auerbach in his *Dante* indicates, Dante's "scene of action" is a concrete one: "What radically distinguishes the *Comedy* from all other visions of the other world is that in it the unity of man's earthly personality is preserved and fixed; the scene of action thus becomes the source of its poetic value, of its infinite truth, of the quality of direct empirical evidence which makes us feel that everything that happens in the work is real and credible and relevant to ourselves. The earthly world is encompassed in the other world of the *Comedy*; true, its historical order and form are destroyed, but in favor of a more complete and final form in which the destroyed form is included." [15]

Dante structures his poem as an interweaving of different systems which correspond to the divine order. There is a physical system dealing with material and scientific phenomena, an ethical system which involves both religious and moral questions, and a historico-political system which treats both the contemporary political situation and historical events and figures.[16] Each of Dante's systems involves a synthesis of different traditions, which compounds the richness of his material and the scholarly achievement of his completed work, an accomplishment which in its thoroughness Papatsonis's poem does not attempt to rival.

Because Dante speaks of salvation for all men in the context of a completely organized Catholic theology, his journey is complicated by a great number of figures, both dammed and blessed, whose function is to illustrate specific theological concepts. Dante is not content merely to present the pilgrimage of the soul, for he turns from the dramatic framework time and again to expound, comment, explain, or pass judgment.[17] The theological progress of the journey is thus made perfectly clear in the *Commedia* through Dante's conversations with Virgil and Beatrice, as well as through the events which befall him and the experiences he undergoes.

In *Ursa Minor*, on the contrary, Papatsonis is completely immersed in the experience of the soul in progress toward a vision of God. Though the poet speaks of "us" in his journey, there are no other identifiable human figures, and the divine agents of the poem are limited to his guide in her many guises and to God, the object of his quest. Subjectively submerged in the mystical process, the poet does not stand aside from the journey either to judge or to explain. Though the pilgrimage is to some extent a trip taken on behalf of the salvation of all men, it is, nevertheless, a more completely personal experience than Dante's trip, less directly related to organized theology than to mystical ecstasy. Lyrical in its expression, *Ursa Minor* does not share with the *Commedia* theological exactness in its description of the progress of the soul. The soul is presented in various states of ecstasy and in varying degrees of awareness. Its acceptance of faith and hope and the final affirmation of love does not occur as a completely logical and progressive revelation. Rather, the work proceeds as a series of uneven mystical experiences which occasionally repeat each other and between which lapses in awareness often occur. *Ursa Minor*, as Papatsonis has himself explained, is more of a confession than a depiction of an action. It must at base be considered, as the poet puts it, a "contemplative diary of my soul's process in the continuous endeavour to acquire a union with the Cosmos, the unknown forces governing the Universe."[18]

From the *Commedia* Papatsonis borrows the use of a woman guide as an active agent in the process of salvation. He takes up a triad of theological values from the eighth sphere of Dante's *Paradiso*, values which he considers central to Dante's vision, and he models his poem on the Dantean journey of man's soul from darkness to light. It is these fundamental similarities between *Ursa Minor* and the *Commedia* which undeniably enrich one's reading of Papatsonis's poem. In spite of often unbreachable differences in theology and technique, the two works can to some extent be considered companions, the more ancient as a parent piece filled with the riches of ages of cultural development from the classical through the medieval, and the more modern as the indebted sibling whose borrowings from the Dantean fount demonstrate the continuing quest in man to reach for the mysteries beyond mere physical existence.

IV *Conclusion*

The influence of Plotinus, St. John of the Cross, and Dante on Papatsonis's poetry are less explicit than they are implicit. Without deliberately modelling on the works of his mentors, Papatsonis's poetry has taken inspiration from selected aspects which have a particular relevance to his own "love-illumed quest" for the divine principle. Convinced that "our soul is a parcel of the universe, and as such immortal," he follows Plotinus in spirit if not in letter of the *Enneads* (the "letter" in this case being virtually impossible of adherence). Plotinus, nevertheless, provides the spine of Papatsonis's pantheism, a spine which in its expression of the chain of being leading to God gives Papatsonis's poetry a unifying transcendent continuity.

In conjunction with the "esoteric psychic stream" of which St. John of the Cross was an exponent, this pantheism finds its most defined shape in the poet's journey to union with the Cosmos. In Papatsonis's journey, one mystical both in content and form, the poet's search for an image of worship and a regaining of his faith is aided by an interceding presence, a sacred examination, divine signs, and, ultimately, a vision of the Divine One Himself; it is a journey which, in the fullness of its religious experience, only Dante could have inspired. But, unlike Dante, Papatsonis is prevented by the mystical process itself from systematic pursuance of theological goals. The mystical influence of all three religious figures seems, in the end, to add up to just this, for it is their mysticism, more than their theology, which makes the most overpowering impact on Papatsonis; and it is this mysticism which most completely dominates the shape of his poetry, leading finally away from canonical or dogmatic niceties.

In Papatsonis's work ideological meanings associated with the passage from sin to salvation only inspire the creation of a dreamlike realm in which the poet can work out the amorphous agony of his soul. Immersed in visionary experiences that have no exact boundaries, no measurable dimensions, Papatsonis finds in Plotinus, St. John of the Cross, and Dante the mystical means to express his metaphysical anguish and the courage to reject the ritual tools which he had used periodically to give a sense of form to his visions.

Notes and References

Chapter One

1. See C. Th. Dimaras, *A History of Modern Greek Literature*, trans. Mary P. Gianos (Albany: State University of New York Press, 1972), pp. 464–467.

2. Linos Politis, *A History of Modern Greek Literature*, trans. Robert Liddell (Oxford: Clarendon Press, 1973), p. 201.

3. *Ibid.*, p. 204

4. *Ibid.*, p. 232

5. *Ibid.*, p. 238.

6. Takis Papatsonis, "O Yperrealismos k' Ego" [Surrealism and I], *Ta Nea Grammata*, 6 (1945), 345. Hereafter referred to as "Surrealism."

7. *Ibid.*, 344.

8. Author's interview with Papatsonis, June 28, 1973.

9. The suggestion was made to Kimon Frair for his original publication of translations of Papatsonis's poems in *Charioteer*, I, No. 3 (1961), and for the later inclusion of those translations in Friar's *Modern Greek Poetry* (New York: Simon and Schuster, 1973).

10. Dimaras, p. 401.

11. Papatsonis, *Askese ston Atho* [An Exercise on Mt. Athos] (Athens: Ikaros, 1963), pp. 117–118.

12. Author's interview with Papatsonis, June 24, 1969.

13. Papatsonis, "K. P. Kavaphes" [C. P. Cavafy], *Semera*, 1 (1933), 133.

14. Papatsonis, "Pyramides" [Pyramids], *Ellenika Phylla*, (Christmas 1936), p. 337.

15. Papatsonis, "E Kritike tou Vivliou" [Book Criticism], *Ellenika Phylla*, 3 (1935), 93.

16. Papatsonis, "Otan Anthise to Amygdalon" [When the Almond Tree Blooms], in *Opou en Kepos* [Where There Is a Garden] (Athens: Philon, 1972), p. 51.

17. Papatsonis, "E Atrote Mousa" [The Invulnerable Muse], in *Opou en Kepos*, p. 93.

18. Papatsonis, "Surrealism," 344.
19. *Ibid.*
20. *Ibid.*, 345
21. Papatsonis, "When the Almond Tree Blooms," p. 93.

Chapter   Two

1. Author's interview with Papatsonis, June 28, 1973.
2. Translations from Dante's *Commedia* are taken from the translation by John Ciardi, *The Inferno* (New York: New American Library, 1954); *The Purgatorio* (New York: New American Library, 1961); *The Paradiso* (New York: New American Library, 1967).

Chapter   Three

1. Letter to the author from Papatsonis, January 7, 1972.
2. Papatsonis, "Chroniko tes Sklavias kai tes Karterias" [Chronicle of Endurance and Suffering], in *Ekloge I* [Selection I] (Athens:Ikaros, 1962), p. 163. Hereafter referred to as "Chronicle."
3. *Ibid.*, p. 165.
4. *Ibid.*, p. 166.
5. *Ibid.*, pp. 165–166.
6. Ernest Beaumont, *The Theme of Beatrice in the Plays of Claudel* (London: Rockliff, 1954), p. 9.
7. Papatsonis, "Chronicle," p. 166.
8. Translations from Ovid's *Metamorphoses* are taken from the translation by Frank Justus Miller, *Metamorphoses* (1916; rpt. Cambridge: Harvard University Press, 1968), I.
9. Papatsonis, "Chronicle," p. 166.
10. John Cuthbert Lawson, *Modern Greek Folklore and Ancient Greek Religion: A Study in Survivals* (1909; rpt. New Hyde Park: University Books, 1964), pp. 163–64.
11. Edith Hamiton, *Mythology* (1940; rpt. New York: New American Library, 1959), pp. 31–32; William King, *Heathen Gods and Heroes* (Carbondale: Southern Illinois University Press, 1965), p. 119; H. J. Rose, *A Handbook of Greek Mythology* (New York: E. P. Dutton and Co., 1959), pp. 112–113.
12. Robert Graves, *The Greek Myths* (Baltimore: Penguin Books, 1955), I, 85.
13. Papatsonis, "Chronicle," p. 166.
14. "The Third Hymn to Aphrodite," *The Homeric Hymns*, trans. Charles Boer (Chicago: Swallow Press, 1970), p. 85.
15. Lawson, pp. 163–164; 171.
16. *Ibid.*, p. 120.
17. Graves, pp. 48–49.

Notes and References

Chapter Four

1. Author's interview with Papatsonis, June 2, 1969.
2. *Ibid.*
3. Papatsonis, "Oi 'Parekvoles' tou Eustathiou Mesa sta Byzantina tous Plaisia" [The "Parekvoles" of Eustathios in their Byzantine Framework], *Tetradio Trito* (1945), p. 71.
4. Kimon Friar, "On Translation," in *Modern Greek Poetry,* pp. 658–659.
5. Papatsonis, "E Kritike tou Vivliou," 93.
6. Papatsonis, "Ena Triptycho apo ton 'Paradeiso' tou Dante" [A Triptych from Dante's *Paradiso*], in *O Tetraperatos Kosmos 1* [The Four Cornered Earth I], p. 202. Hereafter referred to as "Triptych."
7. *Ibid.,* p. 195.
8. Kimon Frair, "Introduction," in *Modern Greek Poetry,* p. 49.
9. Cleon Paraschos, "E Poiese tou Take Papatsone" [The Poetry of Takis Papatsonis], *E Kathemerine,* March 10, 1961, p. 2.
10. Friar, "Introduction," p. 128.
11. *Ibid.*
12. Translations from Plato's *Republic* are taken from the translation by Paul Shorey, *Repubic,* 2 vols. (1935; rpt. Cambridge: Harvard University Press, 1961).
13. Anthony Joseph Mazzeo, *Structure and Thought in the "Paradiso"* (Ithaca: Cornell University Press, 1958), p. 143.
14. See John D. Sinclair, "Note," in *Purgatorio, Divine Comedy of Dante Alighieri,* trans. and ed. John D. Sinclair (1939; rpt. New York: Oxford University Press, 1968), II, 446.

Chapter Five

1. Cleon Paraschos, "The Poetry of Takis Papatsonis," trans. Thomasina Alexander and John Karkas, *The Charioteer,* I, No. 3 (1961), 31.
2. Panayiotis Kanellopoulos, "Poetry and Truth in Neo-Hellenic Life," in *Introduction to Modern Greek Literature,* trans. and ed. Mary Gianos (New York: Twayne Publishers, 1969), p. 31.
3. Translations from Plotinus's *Enneads* are taken from the translation by Stephen Mackenna, *The Enneads,* 2nd ed. (New York: Pantheon Books, 1930).
4. Paraschos, "The Poetry of Takis Papatsonis," 29.
5. *Ibid.,* 1.
6. Kostas Stergiopoulos, "Enas Idiotypos Neoellenas Pistos" [An Original Modern Greek Believer], *Epoches,* No. 5 (September 1963), p. 66.
7. Georgios Themeles, "Papadiamantes-Papatsones" [Papadiamantis-Papatsonis], *E Kathemerine,* February 19, 1963, p. 6.

8. Kostis Palamas, "Akome Enas" [Yet Another], *Empros, February* 25, 1916, p. 1.

9. Papatsonis, "Mythos kai Istoria" [Myth and History], in *Gia Ton Sephere* [For Seferis] (Athens: Ikaros, 1961), p. 27. Hereafter referred to as "Myth."

10. *Ibid.*

11. Translations from St. John of the Cross are taken from the translation by David Lewis, *The Complete Works,* 2 vols., 2nd ed. (London: n.p., 1889–1890).

12. Edmund G. Gardner, *Dante and the Mystics* (1913: rpt. New York: Octagon Books, 1968), p. 300.

13. *Ibid.,* pp. 26–27.

14. Ernst Robert Curtius, *European Literature and the Latin Middle Ages,* trans. Willard R. Trask (New York: Harper and Row, 1953), p. 366.

15. Erich Auerbach, *Dante: Poet of the Secular World,* trans. Ralph Manheim (Chicago: University of Chicago Press, 1961), p. 90.

16. *Ibid.,* p. 101.

17. Jefferson Butler Fletcher, *Dante* (Notre Dame, Indiana: University of Notre Dame Press, n.d.), p. 66.

18. Letter to the author from Papatsonis, June 25, 1968.

Selected Bibliography

The following bibliography is the first to have been collected on the literary works of Takis Papatsonis. In order to be as concise as possible without omitting any newly discovered material, the author has eliminated the titles of all essays printed in *Kathemerine* from 1935 to 1940, the period during which Papatsonis wrote a weekly literary column in that paper, and those which appeared in *Nea Estia*, to which the poet has contributed regularly from 1941 to the present. Both sources have been culled by the poet himself in his selection of essays for his collected works, and the sources themselves are accessible to researchers.

PRIMARY SOURCES

1. Poems

"E Agape Mou" [My Love]. *Akropolis*, July 24, 1914, p. 7.

"Anastasimo" [Resurrectional]. *Eleuthera Grammata*, Nos. 3–4 (1949) p. 101.

"Aneparkeia kai Plesmone" [Insufficiency and Abundance]. *Nea Estia*, 83 (1968), 491.

"Antistrophe tou Lazarou" [The Retortion of Lazarus]. *Emerologion Orizontes* (1942), p. 136.

"To Aprosdoketo Thema" [The Unlooked-For Theme]. *Orizontes*, 1 (1931), 6.

"Asketikon Christougennon" [Ascetic Hymn of Christmas]. *Akropolis*, December 25, 1913, p. 4.

"Asyngnostos" [The Unforgivable]. *Rythmos*, No. 9 (1933), p. 257.

"Athoteta" [Innocence]. *Nea Estia*, 54 (1953), 1010.

"Auto to Anaglypho" [This Relief]. *Kainouria Epoche*, No. 1 (1956), pp. 38–39.

"Deesis" [Supplication]. *Akropolis*, July 20, 1914, p. 1.

"Ekeines oi Enastres Cheimoniatikes Olonychties" [Those Starry Winter Vigils]. *Mousa*, 3 (1923), 140.

Ekloge I [Selection I]. Athens: Ikaros, 1962.

Ekloge II [Selection II]. Athens: Ikaros, 1962.

"Ellesi de Moria" [And to the Greeks Inanity]. *Nea Estia,* 67 (1960), 491–492.

"Enkomion Mnemossynes" [Encomium of a Remembrance]. *E Kathe-merine,*August 14, 1939, p. 3.

"Epigrammata gia Cheimones" [Epigrams for Winters]. *Nea Estia,* 87 (1970), 211–212.

"Epinikeios Paian" [Victory Paean]. *Akropolis,* July 21, 1914, p. 1.

"Eroiko" [Heroic]. *Akropolis,* July 23, 1914, p. 1.

"Euthyne" [Responsibility]. *Nea Estia,* 54 (1953), 1009–1010.

"Exe Poiemata [Six Poems]: 'Iketides' [Suppliants]; 'Megale Anamone tes Epiouses' [Every Day's Great Expectation]; 'Ploia Kai Alla' [The Ships and Other Things]; 'If Only;' 'E Etera Graphe' [The Other Writing]; 'Pros Dysmas' [Westwards]." *O Aionas Mas,* 5 (1951), 34–36.

"Gia ten Anapausi tous sten Anapausi mas" [For their Repose on Our Repose]. *Akropolis,* July 22, 1914, p. 2.

"Goeteia tou Aprile" [April's Enchantment]. *Nea Estia,* 65 (1959), 561.

"Graphe Nesiou" [Island Scroll]. *Nea Estia,* 84 (1968), 1183–1184.

"Gymnasmata se Disticha tes Epoches" [Exercises in Couplets of This Age]. *Athanaika Tetradia,* No. 1 (1950), pp. 3–5.

"Hymnos to Nekron" [Hymn to the Dead]. *Akropolis,* February 22, 1914, p. 2.

"Kai Epi Ges Eirene" [Peace on Earth]. *Akropolis,* November 2, 1913, p. 7.

"Kalanta kai ta Synapta Tous" [Carols and Their Appendices]. *Nea Estia,* 87 (1970), 1–3.

"O Kepouros tou Taphou" [The Grave's Gardener]. *Ellenike Epitheo-resis,* 29 (1936), 83.

"To Karavi" [The Ship]. *Lyra,* Nos. 4–5 (April-May 1919), p. 171.

"To Keri tou Pascha" [Easter Candle]. *Nea Estia,* 63 (1958), 589–590.

"Kleistos Kyklos" [Closed Circle]. *Emerologion Orizontes* (1942), p. 136.

"E Kloste" [The Thread]. *E Peirotike Estia,* 6 (1957), 870–871.

"Megale Tetarte"[Good Wednesday]. *Akropolis,* April 2, 1914, p. 2.

"Ta Metakataklysmaia" [The Metacataclysm]. *Nea Estia,* 87 (1970), 561–563.

"Mimesis Christou" [Imitation of Christ]. *Akropolis,* March 20, 1915, p. 2.

"Nobilissimus Afflictus." *Oi Neoi,* No. 2 (April 1919), pp. 50–51.

"E Olonychtia" [The Vigil]. *Philogike Protochronia* (1958), p. 28.

"Orimotes" [Maturity]. *Mousa,* No. 4 (1923), p. 19.

Selected Bibliography

"Ta Pallekaria" [The Heroes]. *Akropolis,* July 28, 1914, p. 5.
"Pakraormetiko" [Exhortative]. *Akropolis,* July 17, 1914, p. 1.
"Pentekoste" [Pentecost]. *E Kathemerine,* June 13, 1939, p. 3.
"Pisteuo" [I believe]. *Enkyklopaidikon Emerologion* (1957), p. 54.
"Psalmos kai Synapantemata" [Psalms and Encounters]. *Nea Estia,* 73 (1963), 491–493.
"Psichia apo ton Morea tes Diasporas" [Morsels From the Morea of the Diaspora]. *Peloponnesiake Protochronia* (1962), pp. 43–46.
"Seirenes kai Ananke" [Sirens and Necessity]. *Makedonikes Emeres,* 4 (1936), 64.
"Sten Kyra Mou" [To My Lady]. *Akropolis,* August 15, 1914, p. 1.
"Tessara Poiemata [Four Poems]: 'Mythos' [Myth]; 'Tragoudia ton Ephemeron Pragmaton' [Songs of Ephemeral Things]; 'Ta Kleista Ermaria' [The Closed Cupboards]; 'Ta Oreina' [The Mountainous]." *To Trito Mate,* Nos. 4–6 (January–March, 1936), pp. 32–35.
"Thalassinon Orkos" [A Seaman's Oath]. *Akropolis,* July 25, 1914, p. 1.
"Tragoudi gia to Mena Augousto" [A Song for the Month of August]. *Philologike Protochronia* (1955), p. 11.
"O Vasileas Mas" [Our King]. *Akropolis,* July 18, 1914, p. 1.

2. Essays
"The 'Alafroiskiotos' of Sikelianos" [Sikelianos's "Visionary"]. *Angloellenike Epitheorese,* 2 (1946), 240–241.
"Alexandros Papadiamante Erga" [Works of Alexander Papadiamantis]. *Euthyne,* 1 (August, 1961), 63–64.
"Andre Gide." *Semera,* 1 (1933), 159–160.
"Andritzaina" [Andritsena]. *Peloponnesiake Protochronia* (1959), pp. 82–86.
"L'Antinomie dans Creation Valerienne." *L'Hellenisme Contemporain,* No. 1 (1947), pp. 39–41.
Askese ston Atho [An Exercise on Mt. Athos]. *Athens: Ikaros,* 1963.
"Chouan Ramon Chimeneth" [Juan Ramon Jimenez]. *Kainouria Epoche,* No. 4 (1956), pp. 323–325.
"Chronia Polemou" [The War Years]. *Peloponnesiake Protochronia* (1961), pp. 330–333.
"O Demetrios Kapetanakes kai e Ellada" [Demetrios Capetanakis and Greece] *Chronika,* 3 (1945), 269–278.
"Didagma tou Kalou Samareite" [The Teaching of the Good Samaritan]. *Orizontes Ellenikon Emerologion,* (1942), pp. 113–116.
"Elias Venezes" [Elias Venezis] *Kainouria Epoche,* No. 2 (1958), pp. 228–233.
"Ena Elleniko Schedio gia ten Anaviose tes Olympias" [A Greek

Scheme for the Revival of Olympia]. *Ekloge*, 4 (1948), 831–833.
"Ena Mathema ki' ena Poiema" [A Lesson and a Poem]. *Lotos*, No. 3 (Christmas 1968), pp. 4–9.
"Ena Menyma Diavazontas Varnale sto Vouno" [An Interpretation on Reading Varnalis on a Mountain]. *Neoi Stathmoi*, 1 (January, 1959), 9–11.
"Ena Psichion apo Megalo Deipno" [A Morsel from a Great Supper]. *To Trito Mati*, Nos. 4–6 (January-March, 1936), p. 6.
"Enos Chronou Kallitechnia" [A Years's Art]. *Peiraika Grammata*, 1 (October-December, 1940), 37–40.
"Ereuna tou 'Zygou' gia to Eniaio Pneumatiko Kentro" [The Periodical *Zygos's* Research for a Unique Spiritual Center]. *Zygos*, 7 (May-June, 1962), 40.
Ethnegersia: Solomos, Kalvos [National Revolution: Solomos, Calvos]. Athens: Ikaros, 1970.
Friedrich Hölderlins 1770, 1843, 1970. Athens: Ikaros, 1970
"Ge Meter" [Mother Earth]. *Semera*, 1 (1933), 2–5.
"Gerasimou Kasyla: 'Gia ten Eirene' [For Peace]; G. S. Voumblinou: 'Poiemata' [Poems]; E. Skoutare: 'Segana Vemata' [Slow Steps]; Z. Oikonomou: 'O Kosmos ste Dyse tou [The World in its Decline]." *Ellenika Phylla*, 1 (May, 1935), 93.
"Giaponezikoi Kepoi" [Japanese Gardens]. *To Trito Mate*, Nos. 2–3 (November-October, 1935), p. 30.
"Gia to Martzoke" [For Martsokis]. *Phrangelio*, 1 (April 9, 1927), 4.
"Gia to Mpetoben oi Monachikoi Anthropoi" [For Beethoven, the Solitary People]. *Phrangelio*, 1, No. 6 (1927), 15–18.
"E Gnome tes Kritikes" [Criticism's View]. *Ta Nea Grammata*, 6 (1944), 68.
"Hierapostoles" [Missionaries]. *Semera*, 1 (1933), 65–70.
"O Hyperrealismos k' Ego" [Surrealism and I]. *Ta Nea Grammata*, 6 (1945), 340–346.
"E Kallitechnia mas ton Teleutaio Kairo" [Our Art This Last Period]. *Peiraika Grammata*, 2 (1942), 46–47.
"Kavaphes" [Cavafy]. *Nea Techne* (July-October 1942).
"Keltike Techne" [Celtic Art]. *Ellenika Grammata*, 4 (1927), 161–162.
"K. P. Kavaphes" [C. P. Cavafy]. *Semera*, 1 (1933), 132–139.
"Kritike Anthologia gia to Ergo tou Kosta Thyrane" [A Critical Anthology for the Work of Kostas Thyranis]. *Ellenike Demourgia*, 12 (1953), 160.
"E Kritike tou Vivliou" [Book Criticism]. *Ellenika Phylla*, 2 (1935), 28–29; 57–59; 3 (1935), 91–93.
"O Lapathiotes ki' e Semasia tes Diavases" [Lapathiotis and the Meaning of the Passage]. *Orizontes*, 1 (1944), 33.

Selected Bibliography

"Logia tes Ekklesias" [The Words of the Church]. *Orizontes Ellenikon Emerologion* (1943), pp. 339–349.

"Mia dia Martyria" [One for Testimony]. *Semera*, 1 (1933), 156.

"Mnemes Agathon Andron" [Memories of Kind Men]. *Peloponnesiake Protochronia* (1960), pp. 42–44.

Moldovalachika tou Mythou [Moldawalachia in Myth]. Athens: Ikaros, 1965.

"Mythos kai Istoria" [Myth and History]. *Gia ton Sephere*. Athens: Ikaros, 1961. Pp. 24–31.

"Nea Poiemata tou Antrea Kampa apo to Londino" [New Poems of Andreas Kampas from London]. *Kainouria Epoche*, No. 2 (1958), pp. 86–94.

"Odoiporikon Apogeuen eis Romen kai Athenas" [An Account of an Enjoyable Journey in Rome and Athens]. *Katholike*, January 8, 1954, pp. 1; 4; January 15, 1954, p. 1.

Opou en Kepos [Where There Is a Garden]. Athens: Philon, 1972.

"Oi 'Parekvoles' tou Eustathiou Mesa sta Vyzantina tous Plaisia" [The "Parekvoles" of Eustathius in Their Byzantine Framework]. *Tetradio Trito* (1945), pp. 69–72.

"Parisi 1946" [Paris, 1946]. *Kochlias*, 2 (February, 1947), 17–18.

"Pentekosten Eortazomen" [Celebrating Pentecost]. *Katholike*, June 1, 1960, p. 3.

"Piste-Elpida-Agape" [Faith-Hope-Love]. *Peiraika Grammata*, 2 (1942), 309–312.

"Platon kai Valery" [Plato and Valery]. *O Kyklos*, 1 (1945), 14–18.

"Pneuma kai Vivilia sto Elleniko 1942" [Intellect and Books in the Greek 1942]. *E Kathemerine*, February 21, 1943, pp. 1; 2; February 23, 1943, p. 1.

"E Poiese ton Neon: Stephanos Katsampes" [The Poetry of the Young: Stephen Katsambes]. *Orizontes*, 1 (1944), 23.

"O Poietes Edouard Moerike" [The Poet Edouard Moerike]. *Grammata*, No. 3 (1944), pp. 117–118.

"O Poietes Napoleon Lapathiotes" [The Poet Napoleon Lapathiotes]. *Grammata*, No. 7 (1944), pp. 21–22.

"To Provlema" [The Problem]. *Semera*, 2 (1934), 7–10; 29.

"Prologos" [Prologue]. *Dine*. Athens: Ikaros, 1961.

"Propaideia gia ten Kataxe ton 'Vers d'Exil' sto Ergo tou P. Claudel" [Preparation for the Classification of "Vers d' Exil" in the Work of P. Claudel]. *Peiraika Grammata*, 2 (1942), 60–62.

"Skepseis apo to KD Asma tou 'Paradeisou' " [Thoughts from *Paradiso*, Canto XXIV]. *Peiraika Grammata*, 3 (1943), 136–138.

"Symvole se Kritike tou Ergou tou K. Kavaphe" [Advice on the Criticism of Cavafy's Work]. *O Kyklos*, 2 (1932), 87–93.

"Syzetese Pano ste Syngchrone Poiese" [A Discussion on Contemporary Poetry]. *Nea Poreia*, 1 (1955), 365; 369–374.

"O T. Papatsones gia to Mpetoben oi Monachikoi Anthropoi" [T. Papatsonis for Beethoven, the Solitary People]. *Phrangelio*, No. 2 (1927), pp. 15–19.

"T. Papatsone kai K. Sphakianake" [T. Papatsonis and K. Sphakianakis]. *Phrangelio*, No. 1 (January 1928), p. 3.

"Techne kai Kommounismos" [Art and Communism]. *Semera*, 1 (1933), 159.

O Tetraperatos Kosmos I [The Four Cornered Earth I]. Athens: Ikaros, 1966.

"Thrasou Kastanake 'Megaloi Astoi' " [Thrasos Kastanakis "Great Citizens"]. *Ellenika Phylla*, 1 (1935), 28–29.

"Ungaretti: The Great Renovator of Modern Italian Poetry." Trans. Kimon Friar. *Books Abroad*, 44 (1970), 616–617.

SECONDARY SOURCES

"Allelographia k' Hysterographia: T. Papatsone kai K. Sphakianake" [Correspondence and Postcripting: T. Papatsonis and K. Sphakianakis]. *Phrangelio*, No. 1 (January, 1928), p. 16; No. 4 (April, 1928), p. 16; No. 4 (April, 1928), p. 61.

ARGYROPOULOS, GIANKOS. *Chamelophoni Poiese* [Whispered Poetry]. Athens: Estias, n.d.

ARTEMAKE, STELIOS I. "O Papatsones ki' O Kosmos tou" [Papatsonis and His World]. *E Kathemerine*, December 5, 1965, p. 4.

CHATZINES, GIANNES. Rev. of *Askese Ston Athon* [An Exercise on Mt. Athos], by T. K. Papatsonis. *Nea Estia*, 74 (1963), 1319–1321.

———. Rev. of *Moldovalachika tou Mythou* [Moldawalachia in Myth], by T. K. Papatsonis. *Nea Estia*, 79 (1966) 414–415.

———. Rev. of *O Tetraperatos Kosmos I* [The Four Cornered Earth I], by T. K. Papatsonis. *Nea Estia*, 81 (1967), 696–697.

CHOURMOUZIOS, AIM. "T. K. Papatzone: 'Ursa Minor.' " *Nea Estia*, 39 (1946), 55–59.

DELPHES, PHOIBOS. "Pneumatike Aktinovolia sto Ergo tou T. K. Papatsone" [Spiritual Radiance in the work of T. K. Papatsonis]. *Delphika Tetradia*, 3 (1966), 363–364.

DEMAKES, MENAS. "Ta Gegonota kai ta Zetemata: Oi Neoi Akadimaikoi T. K. Papatsones" [The Facts and the Questions: The New Academicians T. K. Papatsonis]. *Nea Estia*, 83 (1968), 55–56.

DEMARAS, C. TH. *A History of Modern Greek Literature*. Trans. Mary Gianos. New York: SUNY, 1972.

Selected Bibliography

FRIAR, KIMON, ed. and trans. *Modern Greek Poetry*. New York: Simon and Schuster, 1973.

GIANNOULOPOULOS, CHRISTOS A. *E Physiolatreia ste Neoellenike Poiese* [The Worship of Nature in Modern Greek Poetry]. Athens: n.p. 1947.

KAMPANES, ARISTOS. "Threskeutikoi Poietai [Religious Poets]. *Ergasia*, 5 (1934), 749.

KARATHANASES, KOSTAS. "Takis Papatsones" [Takis Papatsonis]. *Samiake Epitheorese*, 1 (1964), 104.

MERAKLE, M. G. *E Poiese Mas, O Dichasmos, to Metaichmio* [*Our Poetry, Division, Interval*]. Kalamata: Nestor, 1959.

MYRSIADES, KOSTAS. Rev. of *O Tetraperatos Kosmos I* [The Four Cornered Earth I], by T. K. Papatsonis, *Books Abroad*, 44 (1970), 170–171.

———. "The *Ursa Minor* of Takis Papatsonis and its Dantean Parallels." Disser. Indiana University, 1972.

PALAMAS, K. "Akome Enas" [Yet Another]. *Empros*, February 25, 1916, p. 1.

———. "Meta ton Etsegarau" [After Echegaray]. *Empros*, October 17, 1916, p. 1.

PAPASTAVROS, S. J. "Papatsonis, Takis." *The Penguin Companion to Literature*. Vol. 2. London: Penguin, 1969. P. 594.

PARASCHOS, CLEON. "The Poetry of Takis Papatsonis." Trans. Thomasina Alexander and John Karkas. *The Charioteer*, I, No. 3 (1961), 28–32.

———. *Ellenes Lyrikoi* [Greek Lyricists]. Athens: S. Spyropoulos, 1953.

———. "E Poiese tou Take Papatsone" [The Poetry of Takis Papatsonis]. *E Kathemerine*, March 10, 1961, pp. 1–2.

———. "Revue de l'Annee Litteraire 1938." *L' Hellenisme Contemporain*, 2 (1938), 452–457.

———. "Mia Matia sto Syngchrono Neoelleniko Lyrismo" [A Glance at Contemporary Greek Poetry]. *Semera*, 1 (1933), 368–370.

———. Rev. of *Ekloge I*, by T. K. Papatsonis. *Nea Estia*, 16 (1934), 619–621.

POLITES, LINOS. *A History of Modern Greek Literature*. Trans. Robert Liddell. Oxford: Clarendon Press, 1973.

STATHOPOULOS, DEM. L. "To Photeinotero Pragma" [The Brightest Thing]. *E Kathemerine*, May 26, 1965, p. 5.

STERGIOPOULOS, KOSTAS. "Enas Idiotypos Neoellenas Pistos" [An Original Modern Greek Believer]. *Epoches*, No. 5 (September 1963), p. 66.

THEMELE, G. "Papadiamantes-Papatsones" [Papadiamantis-Papatsonis]. *E Kathemerine*, February 19, 1963, pp. 1, 6.

THEOTOKES, GIORGOS. "Oi Kindymoi tou Mystikismou" [The Dangers of Mysticism]. *O Kyklos*, 1 (1932), 242–253.

THRYLOS, ALKES. Rev. of *Anabase and Tamerlanos*, trans. by T. K. Papatsonis. *Kainouria Epoche*, No. 4 (1957).

———. Rev. of *Ekloge II* [Selection II], by T. K. Papatsonis. *Kainouria Epoche*, No. 3 (1963), p. 268.

"Ursa Minor." *Kochlias*, No. 4 (March, 1946), p. 72.

VARNALES, K. "Threskeutikos Logos" [A Religious Word]. *Proia*, January 5, 1943, p. 3.

VOUTIERIDE, ELIA P. *Historia tes Neoellenikes Logotechnias: 1000–1930, 1930–1965* [A History of Modern Greek Literature: 1000–1930, 1930–1965]. 2nd ed. Athens: Papadema, 1965.

Index

Index

Index